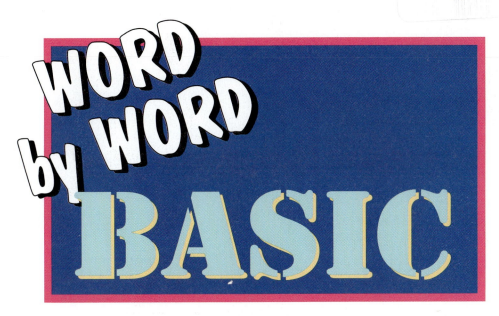

WORD by WORD BASIC

Beginning Workbook

Steven J. Molinsky · Bill Bliss

Contributing Author
Elizabeth Handley

Longman

Publisher: Louisa B. Hellegers
Electronic Production and Page Composition: Jan Sivertsen
Manufacturing Manager: Ray Keating
Art Director: Merle Krumper
Interior Design: Kenny Beck and Jan Sivertsen
Cover Design: Joel Mitnick Design/Merle Krumper

Illustrations: Richard E. Hill

The authors gratefully acknowledge the contribution of Tina Carver
in the development of the *Word by Word* program.

Printed in the United States of America

10

ISBN 0-13-278516-1

CONTENTS

A. WHAT'S THE WORD?

Mary Beth Anderson

last	first	middle

1. My _____first_____ name is Mary.
2. My _____ name is Beth.
3. My _____ name is Anderson.

(216) 898-9575

telephone	area

4. My _____ code is 216.
5. My _____ number is 898-9575.

15 Central Street #3
Cleveland, OH 44107

apartment	address	city	state	zip

6. My _____ is 15 Central Street.
7. My _____ is Cleveland.
8. My _____ is Ohio.
9. My _____ number is 3.
10. My _____ code is 44107.

B. WHAT'S THE ANSWER?

_b_ 1. What's your first name?
___ 2. And your last name?

a. Montero
b. Carlos

___ 3. What's your address?
___ 4. What city?
___ 5. What's your zip code?

c. 90027
d. 629 Parkside Avenue
e. Los Angeles

___ 6. What's your phone number?
___ 7. What's your social security number?

f. 204-37-1958
g. 354-8909

Circle the correct answer.

1. (John)   Boston
2. 625-3067   3B
3. Texas   Dallas
4. Miami   13 Maple Drive
5. 11375   CA
6. 212   Brooklyn

D. YOUR APPLICATION

Fill in the form with your personal information.

NAME:	_____		
	FIRST	MIDDLE	LAST
ADDRESS:	_____		
	NUMBER STREET		APT. NUMBER
	_____		
	CITY	STATE	ZIP CODE
TELEPHONE:	_____		

E. YOUR FRIEND'S APPLICATION

Interview a friend. Fill in the form with your friend's personal information.

NAME:	_____		
	FIRST	MIDDLE	LAST
ADDRESS:	_____		
	NUMBER STREET		APT. NUMBER
	_____		
	CITY	STATE	ZIP CODE
TELEPHONE:	_____		

A. WHO ARE THEY?

granddaughter	grandfather	husband	mother	sister	son

1. wife and _____husband_____

2. _____ and father

3. daughter and _____

4. _____ and brother

5. grandmother and _____

6. _____ and grandson

B. MATCHING: *WHO ARE THEY?*

_c_ **1.** mother and father   **a.** children

___ **2.** son and daughter   **b.** grandparents

___ **3.** grandson and granddaughter   **c.** parents

___ **4.** grandmother and grandfather   **d.** grandchildren

C. WHICH WORD?

1. Who is he?   He's my (mother (father)).

2. Who is she?   She's my (sister   brother).

3. Who is he?   He's my (son   daughter).

4. Her name is Alice.   She's my (husband   wife).

5. His name is Peter.   He's my (grandson   granddaughter).

6. His name is George.   He's my (sister   brother).

7. Who are they?   They're my (grandson   grandchildren).

D. HIS OR HER?

1. What's your grandson's name?   __His__ name is Tommy.
2. What's your wife's name?   _____ name is Irene.
3. What's your daughter's name?   _____ name is Karen.
4. What's your brother's name?   _____ name is Eduardo.
5. What's your mother's name?   _____ name is Ellen.
6. What's your husband's name?   _____ name is Michael.

E. MEET OUR FAMILY

brother	daughter	granddaughter	grandson	son	wife

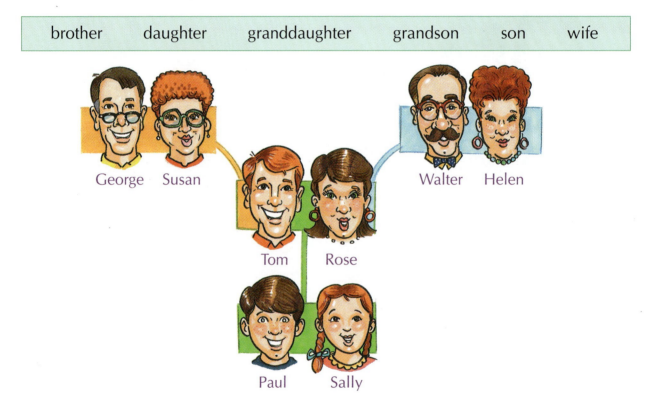

George Susan   Tom   Rose   Walter Helen

Paul   Sally

1. Tom and Rose are husband and
   _____wife_____.

2. Rose and Sally are mother and
   _____.

3. Tom and Paul are father and
   _____.

4. Sally and Paul are sister and
   _____.

5. George and Paul are grandfather and
   _____.

6. Helen and Sally are grandmother and
   _____.

F. TELL ABOUT YOUR FAMILY

1. _____ is my mother.
2. _____ is my father.
3. _____ is my . . . .
4. _____ is my . . . .
5. _____ is my . . . .
6. _____ is my . . . .

A. WHO ARE THEY?

| father-in-law | niece | sister-in-law | son-in-law | uncle |

1. aunt and __uncle__

2. _____ and nephew

3. mother-in-law and _____

4. daughter-in-law and _____

5. _____ and brother-in-law

B. MEET OUR FAMILY

| brother | daughter-in-law | nephew | niece | sister-in-law | son | son-in-law | uncle |

Dan   Lois

Bill   Anna

Frank   Sarah

Kate   Richard

Peter   Jane

1. Lois and Frank are mother and
_____son_____ .

2. Anna and Frank are sister and
_____ .

3. Anna and Jane are aunt and
_____ .

4. Jane and Bill are niece and
_____ .

5. Sarah and Richard are aunt and
_____ .

6. Lois and Sarah are mother-in-law and
_____ .

7. Dan and Bill are father-in-law and
_____ .

8. Bill and Sarah are brother-in-law and
_____ .

A. WHICH ROOM?

Put the activity in the room where it belongs.

brush my teeth	eat dinner	go to bed	make the bed	take a shower
cook dinner	floss my teeth	have lunch	shave	wash my face
eat breakfast	get up	make breakfast	sleep	

- _brush my teeth_
- _____
- _____
- _____
- _____

- _____
- _____
- _____
- _____

- _____
- _____
- _____
- _____

B. CHECKLIST: *WHAT DO YOU DO EVERY DAY?*

Check the things you do every day.

___ get up   ___ shave   ___ make breakfast
___ take a bath   ___ put on makeup   ___ eat breakfast
___ take a shower   ___ brush my hair   ___ make lunch
___ wash my face   ___ comb my hair   ___ have lunch
___ brush my teeth   ___ get dressed   ___ cook dinner
___ floss my teeth   ___ make the bed   ___ eat dinner

C. WHICH WORD?

1. I comb my ((hair) teeth).
2. I put on (my face   makeup).
3. I go to (bed   bath).
4. I eat (teeth   dinner).
5. I have (lunch   sleep).
6. I get (bed   dressed).

7. I (floss   wash) my face.
8. I (shave   have) breakfast.
9. I (brush   wash) my teeth.
10. I (get   go) undressed.
11. I (make   take) a shower.
12. I (make   take) the bed.

A. WHICH WORD?

1. He's (reading (feeding)) the cat.

2. I'm (listening to   watching) the radio.

3. My mother is (ironing   sweeping) the floor.

4. I'm (practicing   doing) the guitar.

5. My father is (dusting   doing) the laundry.

6. My sister is (washing   walking) the dishes.

B. WHAT'S THE ACTION?

| ironing | playing | reading | feeding |

1. ____feeding____ : the dog   the cat   the baby
2. _____ : a book   a newspaper   a textbook
3. _____ : a shirt   a blouse   a dress
4. _____ : the piano   the guitar   basketball

C. CROSSWORD

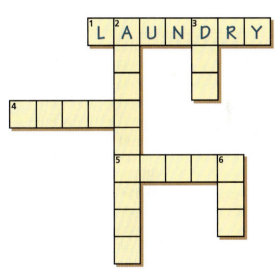

```
1 L A U N D R Y
```

ACROSS

1. I'm doing the _____. My shirts are dirty.

4. They're sweeping the _____.

5. He's listening to _____.

DOWN

2. Jane is cleaning her _____. She's vacuuming and dusting.

3. Susan is walking the _____.

6. I'm going to feed the _____.

A. WHICH WORD?

1. There's a ((globe) map) next to the (pen pencil) sharpener.
2. There's a (computer calculator) next to the bookshelf.

3. There's a (notebook textbook) on the teacher's (aide desk).
4. The graph (paper projector) and (clock chalk) are next to the book.

5. The teacher is at the (board screen).
6. The (ruler eraser) is on the chalk (shelf tray).

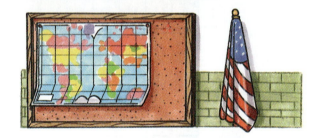

7. There's a (map book) on the bulletin board.
8. There's a (flag globe) next to the bulletin board.

9. There's a ruler on the (chair desk).
10. There's a (clock PA system) on the wall.

B. MATCHING: *WHAT'S THE WORD?*

Draw a line to complete the word. Then write the word on the line.

1. note   tack   _____notebook_____
2. thumb   book   _____
3. loud   shelf   _____
4. book   speaker   _____

C. CROSSWORD

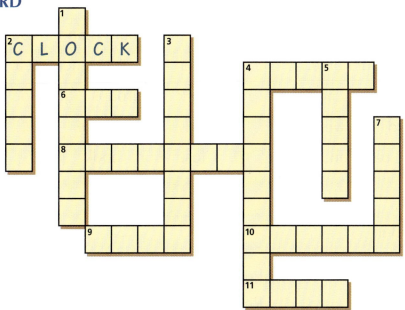

ACROSS

2.

4.

6.

8.

9.

10.

11.

DOWN

1.

2.

3.

4.

5.

7.

D. WHAT'S IN YOUR CLASSROOM?

In my classroom there's . . .

___ a clock	___ an eraser	___ a pencil sharpener
___ a board	___ a flag	___ a bookshelf
___ a bulletin board	___ a globe	___ a computer
___ chalk	___ a map	___ a slide projector

A. WHICH WORD?

1. Stand (up   down).
2. (Raise   Write) your name.
3. Erase your (name   teacher).
4. Go to the (board   answer).
5. (Raise   Read) page ten.
6. Put away your (hand   book).
7. Listen to the (teacher   seat).
8. Work in (groups   questions).
9. Study (seat   page) nine.
10. Close your (book   page).

B. OUT OF ORDER!

Put the actions in order.

___ Go to the board.
_1_ Stand up.
___ Erase your name.
___ Write your name.
___ Sit down.

___ Put your book away.
___ Read page one.
___ Close your book.
_1_ Open your book.
___ Read page two.

1.

2.

C. YOU'RE THE TEACHER!

Write sentences with these words.

Close Erase Open Put away Read Write	your	answer. book. name. question.

1. _____Close your book._____
2. _____
3. _____
4. _____
5. _____
6. _____
7. _____
8. _____
9. _____
10. _____
11. _____
12. _____

A. WHAT'S THE ACTION?

Circle the correct answer.

1. (Correct (Collect)) the tests.

2. (Take   Do) notes.

3. (Bring in   Go over) your homework.

4. (Check   Hand in) your homework.

5. (Answer   Correct) your mistakes.

6. (Take out   Pass out) a piece of paper.

7. (Turn off   Lower) the shades.

8. (Watch   Go over) the answers.

B. LISTENING: *WHAT'S THE WORD?*

Listen and circle the words you hear.

1. (Pass out)   Take out
2. Go over   Lower
3. Check   Take

4. Correct   Collect
5. Turn on   Turn off
6. Go over   Do over

A. WHERE DO THEY LIVE?

apartment building condominium farmhouse mobile home
cabin dormitory houseboat nursing home

1. I live in a ___condominium___ .

2. We live in a _____ .

3. We live in a _____ .

4. I live in an _____ .

5. We live in a _____ .

6. I live in a _____ .

7. I live in a _____ .

8. I live in a _____ .

B. MATCHING

_d_ 1. a house for two families   **a.** houseboat
___ 2. a mobile home   **b.** shelter
___ 3. a building for students   **c.** farmhouse
___ 4. a house on a farm   **d.** duplex
___ 5. a house on water   **e.** nursing home
___ 6. a house for old people   **f.** trailer
___ 7. a place for an emergency   **g.** dormitory

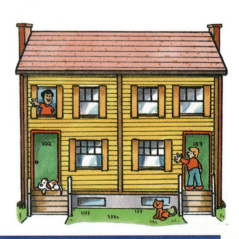

A. WHERE ARE THEY?

Look at page 20 of the Basic Picture Dictionary. Complete the sentences.

coffee table	end table	mantel	photograph	speaker	television
curtains	lamp	painting	pillow	stereo	VCR

1. There's a _____lamp_____ on the end table.

2. There's an _____ next to the couch.

3. There's a _____ on the couch.

4. There's a _____ on the rug.

5. There's a _____ on the wall.

6. There's a _____ on the bookcase.

7. There's a _____ on the fireplace.

8. There are _____ on the window.

9. There's a _____ system,

   a _____, a _____,

   and a _____ in the wall unit.

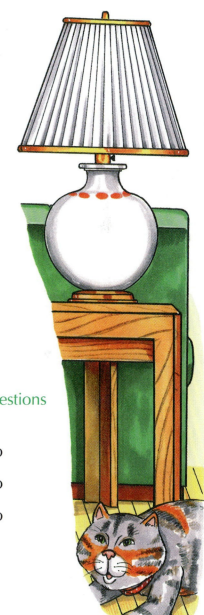

B. LISTENING: *YES OR NO?*

Look at page 20 of the Basic Picture Dictionary. Listen to the questions and circle *Yes* or *No*.

1. (Yes)   No   4. Yes   No   7. Yes   No

2. Yes   No   5. Yes   No   8. Yes   No

3. Yes   No   6. Yes   No   9. Yes   No

C. WHICH WORD DOESN'T BELONG?

1. armchair   (end table)   loveseat   sofa
2. mantel   fireplace   bookcase   fireplace screen
3. lampshade   curtains   window   drapes
4. television   stereo system   VCR   plant
5. picture   photograph   pillow   painting
6. wall   speaker   floor   ceiling

A. WHERE ARE THEY?

Look at page 22 of the Basic Picture Dictionary. Write the words where they belong.

butter dish	coffee pot	pitcher	serving bowl	tablecloth
candlestick	creamer	salad bowl	serving platter	teapot
centerpiece	pepper shaker	salt shaker	sugar bowl	

On the buffet:

- _____pitcher_____
- _____
- _____
- _____

On the serving cart:

- _____
- _____
- _____
- _____

On the table:

- _____
- _____
- _____
- _____
- _____
- _____

B. MATCHING: *WHERE ARE THEY?*

Look at page 22 of the Basic Picture Dictionary. Complete these sentences.

_e_ **1.** The salad bowl is   **a.** next to the creamer.

___ **2.** The sugar bowl is   **b.** next to the pepper shaker.

___ **3.** The candlestick is   **c.** next to the serving platter.

___ **4.** The serving bowl is   **d.** next to the centerpiece.

___ **5.** The salt shaker is   **e.** next to the pitcher.

C. MATCHING: *WHAT'S THE WORD?*

Draw a line to complete the word. Then write the word on the line.

1. candle   pot   _____candlestick_____

2. table   piece   _____

3. tea   cloth   _____

4. center   stick   _____

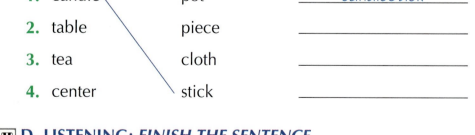

D. LISTENING: *FINISH THE SENTENCE*

Listen and choose the correct word.

1. (dish)   bowl   **3.** pitcher   picture   **5.** coffee pot   teapot

2. buffet   bowl   **4.** platter   shaker   **6.** centerpiece   creamer

A. FINISH THE PLACE SETTING

| butter knife | cup | dinner fork | salad plate | soup bowl | teaspoon |

1. The ___teaspoon___ goes between the knife and the soup spoon.

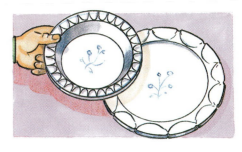

2. The _____ goes on the dinner plate.

3. The _____ goes to the left of the dinner plate.

4. The _____ goes on the saucer.

5. The _____ goes to the left of the bread-and-butter plate.

6. The _____ goes on the bread-and-butter plate.

B. WHICH WORDS ARE CORRECT?

Circle the correct words.

1. (dinner) / (salad) / butter   fork

2. saucer / salad / dinner   plate

3. soup   saucer / bowl / spoon

15

A. MATCHING: *WHERE ARE THEY?*

Look at page 26 of the Basic Picture Dictionary. Complete the sentences.

_d_ 1. The alarm clock is
___ 2. The jewelry box is
___ 3. The pillowcase is
___ 4. The blanket is
___ 5. The quilt is
___ 6. The blinds are

a. on the pillow.
b. on the bedspread.
c. on the dresser.
d. on the night table.
e. on the window.
f. on the sheet.

B. WHICH WORD DOESN'T BELONG?

1. dresser	chest of drawers	bureau	footboard
2. day bed	nightstand	twin bed	cot
3. bunk bed	convertible sofa	water bed	comforter
4. blanket	pillowcase	quilt	electric blanket
5. headboard	mattress	jewelry box	box spring
6. blinds	sheet	pillow	bedspread

C. LISTENING: *WHICH ROOM?*

Listen and circle the letter of the room these people are talking about.

A

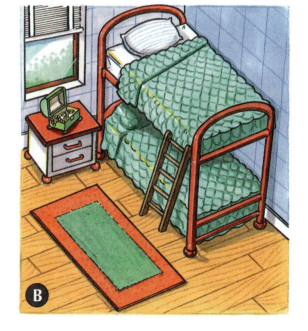

B

1. A (B)   3. A B   5. A B   7. A B
2. A B   4. A B   6. A B   8. A B

A. WHICH GROUP?

cookbook	garbage disposal	pot scrubber	scouring pad	stove
dish towel	microwave	potholder	sink	toaster
dishwasher detergent	oven	range	sponge	

These are for cleaning:

- _dishwasher detergent_
- _____
- _____
- _____
- _____
- _____
- _____

These are for cooking:

- _cookbook_
- _____
- _____
- _____
- _____
- _____
- _____

B. WHICH WORD?

Look at page 28 of the Basic Picture Dictionary. Circle the correct answer.

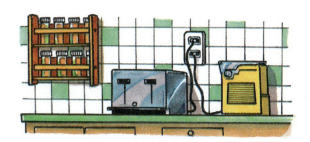

1. There's a ((spice) dish) rack on the wall.

2. The garbage (pail   disposal) is under the sink.

3. There's a (potholder   pot scrubber) next to the sink.

4. The (dishwasher   oven) door is open.

5. There's a (canister   can opener) next to the toaster.

6. There are two (placemats   potholders) on the kitchen table.

7. There's a cookbook on the (counter   cabinet).

8. The ice maker and the ice (rack   tray) are in the (freezer   faucet).

C. WHICH WORD DOESN'T BELONG?

1. freezer	ice maker	(faucet)	ice tray
2. garbage pail	canister	trash compactor	garbage disposal
3. sponge	scouring pad	pot scrubber	sink
4. microwave	potholder	oven	toaster
5. toaster	can opener	dish rack	microwave

A. WHICH GROUP?

baby carrier	booster seat	doll	mobile	rattle	stuffed animal	teddy bear
baby seat	car seat	high chair	playpen	stroller	swing	walker

Places where the baby sits:

- _baby carrier_
- _____
- _____
- _____
- _____

- _____
- _____
- _____
- _____

Things the baby plays with:

- _____
- _____
- _____
- _____
- _____

B. MATCHING: *WHERE ARE THEY?*

Look at page 30 of the Basic Picture Dictionary. Complete the sentences.

_e_ **1.** The doll is
___ **2.** The teddy bear is
___ **3.** The diaper pail is
___ **4.** The swing is
___ **5.** The stuffed animal is
___ **6.** The night light is
___ **7.** The baby is

a. in the crib.
b. next to the changing table.
c. in the playpen.
d. on the chest of drawers.
e. in the toy chest.
f. between the toy chest and the playpen.
g. between the crib and the changing table.

C. LISTENING

Listen and choose the correct picture.

1. _____ _____ ✓ 2. _____ _____ 3. _____ _____

4. _____ _____ 5. _____ _____ 6. _____ _____

BABY CARE

A. WHERE DO THEY GO?

baby lotion baby powder formula nipple ointment pacifier teething ring vitamins

These go in the baby's mouth:

- _____ formula _____
- _____
- _____
- _____
- _____

These go on the baby's body:

- _____
- _____
- _____

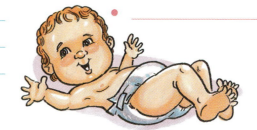

B. WHAT'S THE WORD?

baby food	baby shampoo	cotton swabs	formula	pins
baby powder	bib	disposable	nipple	teething ring

1. The baby is hungry. Put some _____ formula _____ in her bottle.
   Now put a _____ on the bottle.

2. The baby is getting new teeth. She needs a _____.

3. I'm going to wash the baby's hair. Where's the _____?

4. The baby's ears are dirty. We need some _____.

5. Joey is hungry. We need some more _____.

6. Put a _____ on the baby. She's going to eat.

7. We don't need any diaper _____ because we use _____ diapers.

8. Put some _____ on the baby when you change his diaper.

C. LISTENING: *WHICH BABY?*

Listen and decide which baby they're talking about.

(A) (B)

1. (A)   B   3. A   B   5. A   B   7. A   B
2. A   B   4. A   B   6. A   B   8. A   B

THE BATHROOM

BASIC DICTIONARY
pages 34–35

A. MATCHING: *WHERE ARE THEY?*

Look at page 34 of the Basic Picture Dictionary. Complete the sentences.

_e_	**1.** The man is	**a.** over the sink.
___	**2.** The drain is	**b.** next to the toilet.
___	**3.** The towels are	**c.** in the bathtub.
___	**4.** The sponge is	**d.** on top of the vanity.
___	**5.** The mirror is	**e.** on the scale.
___	**6.** The sink is	**f.** next to the shower curtain.
___	**7.** The plunger is	**g.** on the towel rack.

B. WHICH WORD?

1. I clean the toilet with a (plunger (toilet brush)).

2. Wash the bathtub with the (sponge   bath mat).

3. I use the (air freshener   hair dryer) after I wash my hair.

4. Put the aspirin in the (medicine chest   wastebasket).

5. Use the (scale   Water Pik) when you brush your teeth.

6. I look in the (mirror   vanity) when I brush my hair.

7. Put the (rubber mat   bath mat) in the bathtub.

C. WHICH WORDS ARE CORRECT?

Circle the correct words.

1. medicine (cabinet) mirror (chest)

2. rubber bath towel mat

3. toilet freshener seat paper

D. LISTENING: *FINISH THE SENTENCE*

Listen and choose the correct answer.

1. (hamper)   plunger   **4.** freshener   dispenser

2. brush   cabinet   **5.** shower curtain   hair dryer

3. bathtub   bath mat   **6.** rubber mat   towel rack

A. WHERE DO THEY GO?

Put the products where they belong.

after shave lotion	conditioner	hairspray	razor blades	toothbrush
brush	dental floss	mouthwash	shampoo	toothpaste
comb	electric razor	razor	shaving creme	

Hair care products:

- _____brush_____
- _____
- _____
- _____
- _____

Dental care products:

- _____
- _____
- _____
- _____

Shaving products:

- _____
- _____
- _____
- _____

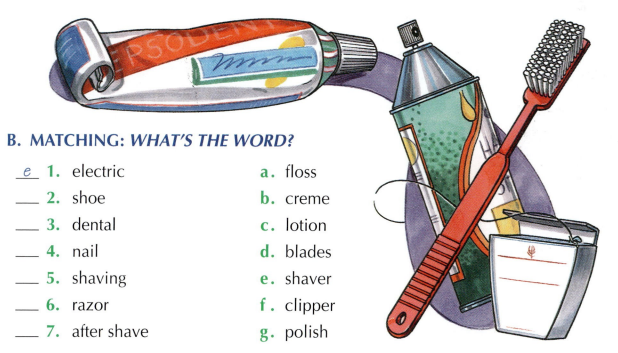

B. MATCHING: *WHAT'S THE WORD?*

_e_	**1.** electric	**a.**	floss
___	**2.** shoe	**b.**	creme
___	**3.** dental	**c.**	lotion
___	**4.** nail	**d.**	blades
___	**5.** shaving	**e.**	shaver
___	**6.** razor	**f.**	clipper
___	**7.** after shave	**g.**	polish

C. LISTENING

Listen and circle the word you hear.

1.	(nail polish)	nail clipper	**4.**	hairspray	razor blades
2.	mouthwash	dental floss	**5.**	shoe polish	shampoo
3.	toothpaste	toothbrush	**6.**	electric razor	electric shaver

D. WHICH WORD IS CORRECT?

Circle the correct words.

1. shoe | **polish** / spray
2. shaving / shower | cap
3. nail | clipper / powder
4. dental | stick / floss

E. CROSSWORD

ACROSS

3.
5.
8.

9.
11.
12.

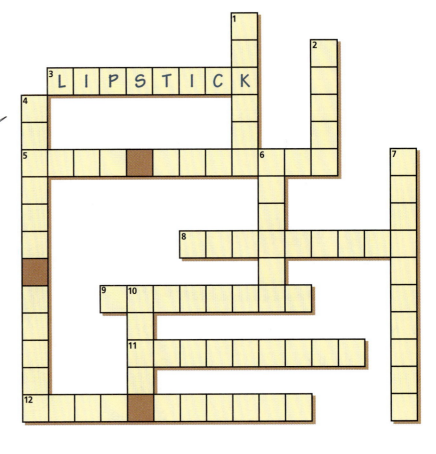

DOWN

1.

2.

4.

6.

7.

10.

A. MATCHING: *WHERE ARE THEY?*

Look at page 38 of the Basic Picture Dictionary. Complete the sentences.

_f_ 1. The clothespins are   a. in the bucket.

___ 2. The sponge is   b. next to the dustpan.

___ 3. The trash can is   c. in front of the utility sink.

___ 4. The scrub brush is   d. in front of the washer and dryer.

___ 5. The laundry basket is   e. on the utility sink.

___ 6. The broom is   f. on the clothesline.

B. WHICH WORD?

1. I'm going to do the laundry. Where's the laundry (bucket (basket))?

2. The (ironing board   iron) is hot. I can iron my shirt now.

3. I'm going to dust the floor with a (dustpan   mop).

4. Turn on the (vacuum   iron) and clean the rug.

5. It's warm and sunny. I'm going to dry my clothes on the (clothesline   dryer).

6. Throw the old bottles in the (garbage can   recycling bin). Don't use the trash can.

C. WHICH WORDS ARE CORRECT?

Circle the correct words.

1. Clean the floor with a   broom (vacuum) pail .

2. Turn on the   iron clothespins vacuum .

3. Open the   dryer dustpan trash can .

4. Wash the sink with a   mop sponge scrub brush .

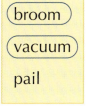

D. LISTENING: *YES OR NO?*

Look at page 38 of the Basic Picture Dictionary. Listen to the question and circle *Yes* or *No*.

1. Yes (No)   3. Yes No   5. Yes No   7. Yes No

2. Yes No   4. Yes No   6. Yes No   8. Yes No

A. WHAT'S THE WORD?

Look at page 40 of the Basic Picture Dictionary. Complete the sentences.

deck doorbell driveway lamppost patio shutters tool shed TV antenna

1. There's a _____lamppost_____ next to the mailbox.

2. There's a _____ next to the front door.

3. There's a _____ on the roof, next to the chimney.

4. There are _____ on three front windows.

5. A man is standing in the _____ .

6. There are two chairs and a table on the _____ .

7. There's a chair and a barbecue on the _____ .

8. A man is sitting next to the _____ .

B. MATCHING: *THEY GO TOGETHER*

_e_ 1. mailbox   a. TV

___ 2. driveway   b. window

___ 3. satellite dish   c. chicken

___ 4. barbecue   d. roof

___ 5. shutter   e. letter

___ 6. chimney   f. grass

___ 7. lawnmower   g. car

C. WHICH WORD?

1. There are two letters in the (lamppost (mailbox)).

2. Put the car in the (garage   tool shed).

3. I like to eat dinner outside on the (deck   satellite dish).

4. Who is at the door? I hear the (lawnmower   doorbell).

5. I'm going to put some chairs on the front (door   porch).

6. Are you going to cook dinner on the (chimney   barbecue)?

7. I can't see out the window when you close the (shutters   back door).

8. We can watch a lot of TV programs because we have a (satellite dish   patio).

A. WHICH WORD?

1. Throw the garbage down the ((chute)   peephole).

2. Use the (lock   buzzer) and the door chain when you close the door.

3. Put these boxes in the (mailbox   storage room).

4. Is there a (whirlpool   smoke detector) in the kitchen?

5. The air conditioner is broken. Call the (intercom   superintendent).

6. I'm going downstairs to the (lobby   balcony) to get the mail.

7. It's very hot in here. Turn on the (fire alarm   air conditioner).

B. MY APARTMENT BUILDING

air conditioner	intercom	parking garage
balcony	laundry room	peephole
buzzer	lobby	pool
elevator		superintendent

I live in a large apartment house. When my friends visit, they ring the

_____buzzer_____ [1] in the _____ [2] and they say "hello" on the

_____ [3]. Then they take the _____ [4] to my apartment on the fifth floor.

I always look through the _____ [5] before I open the door.

When it's warm and sunny, we like to sit outside on the _____ [6]. When

it's hot, we turn on the _____ [7] or we go swimming in the _____ [8].

I like my apartment building very much. There's a _____ [9] for

washing clothes, and there's a _____ [10] for my car. Also, there's a wonderful

_____ [11] in the building who fixes everything!

C. LISTENING

Listen and circle the word you hear.

1. (intercom)   alarm
2. lobby   laundry
3. lock   lot
4. garage   garbage
5. peephole   pool
6. garbage   storage

HOUSING UTILITIES, SERVICES, AND REPAIRS

A. WHO ARE THEY?

Look at page 44 of the Basic Picture Dictionary. Complete the sentences.

appliance repair person	electrician	handyman	plumber
carpenter	exterminator	locksmith	TV repair person
chimney sweep	gardener	painter	

A lot of people are working at this house today. The ___chimney sweep___ [1] is working

on the roof. The _____ [2] is in the bathroom. The _____ [3] is painting

the bedroom. The _____ [4] is fixing the refrigerator. The

_____ [5] is in the living room. The _____ [6], the

_____ [7], and the _____ [8] are working in the basement.

The _____ [9] is fixing the door. The _____ [10] is planting a tree

in the yard. The _____ [11] is also outside. He's fixing the stairs.

B. WHO SHOULD THEY CALL?

Tell these people who they should call.

My TV is broken.

I need a new lock on my door.

1. Call the ___TV repair person___ . 2. Call the _____ .

My chimney is very dirty.

My toilet is broken.

3. Call the _____ . 4. Call the _____ .

I have cockroaches in my apartment.

I want a yellow kitchen.

5. Call the _____ . 6. Call the _____ .

I need some new stairs.

I need some small repairs.

7. Call the _____ . 8. Call the _____ .

A. WHAT'S THE TOOL?

1. hammer   a.   b.   c.

2. saw   a.   b.   c.

3. pliers   a.   b.   c.

4. bolt   a.   b.   c.

5. rake   a.   b.   c.

6. nail   a.   b.   c.

B. WHICH WORD?

1. I'm going to water the garden with the (hose washer).
2. I want to plant these flowers. I need a (paint roller shovel).
3. I can't see. Please turn on the (flashlight electric drill).
4. Put the leaves in the (toolbox wheelbarrow).
5. You can cut the wood with this (hammer saw).
6. Turn the bolt with a (wrench screwdriver).
7. Hammer the (nail screw) into the wood.

C. MATCHING: *WHAT'S THE WORD?*

Draw a line to complete the word. Then write the word on the line.

1. screw   mower   _screwdriver_
2. flash   paper   _____
3. paint   light   _____
4. sand   driver   _____
5. wheel   brush   _____
6. lawn   barrow   _____

D. WHICH WORD DOESN'T BELONG?

1. shovel   rake   (paint roller)   lawnmower
2. hammer   saw   electric drill   step ladder
3. screw   vise   nail   bolt
4. hose   wrench   screwdriver   pliers
5. bolt   nut   sandpaper   washer

E. CROSSWORD

ACROSS

1.

11.

4.

12.

6.

13.

9.

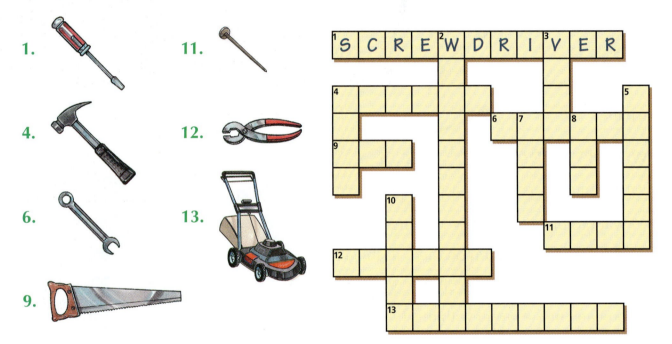

S C R E W D R I V E R

DOWN

2.

5.

8.

3.

7.

10.

4.

A. MATCHING

_c_ **1.** one
2. ten
3. one hundred
4. one thousand

a. 10
b. 1000
c. 1
d. 100

___ **5.** eight
___ **6.** eighteen
___ **7.** eighty
___ **8.** eight hundred

e. 800
f. 80
g. 8
h. 18

B. WHAT'S THE NUMBER?

1. six _____6_____
2. twelve _____
3. eighteen _____
4. fifteen _____
5. forty _____
6. ninety _____

7. twenty-five _____
8. thirty-three _____
9. seventy-two _____
10. sixty-seven _____
11. two hundred _____
12. one thousand _____

C. WHAT'S THE WORD?

1 _____one_____
5 _____
8 _____
11 _____
17 _____

20 _____
30 _____
56 _____
94 _____
100 _____

D. LISTENING: *CIRCLE THE NUMBER*

Listen and circle the number you hear.

1. 13 (30)
2. 14 40
3. 15 50
4. 16 60
5. 17 70

6. 18 80
7. 19 90
8. 35 45
9. 56 66
10. 11 21

A. MATCHING

_b_ **1.** third   **a.** 30th   ___ **5.** first   **e.** 21st

___ **2.** thirteenth   **b.** 3rd   ___ **6.** second   **f.** 12th

___ **3.** thirtieth   **c.** 33rd   ___ **7.** twelfth   **g.** 1st

___ **4.** thirty-third   **d.** 13th   ___ **8.** twenty-first   **h.** 2nd

B. WHAT'S THE NUMBER?

1. first   _1st_   **6.** thirty-third   _____

2. eleventh   _____   **7.** sixteenth   _____

3. seventh   _____   **8.** sixtieth   _____

4. second   _____   **9.** fifty-ninth   _____

5. forty-fourth   _____   **10.** ninety-fifth   _____

C. LISTENING: *WHERE DO THEY LIVE?*

Listen and circle the number you hear.

1. 8th   (18th)   **5.** 22nd   27th

2. 4th   40th   **6.** 106th   105th

3. 31st   33rd   **7.** 8th   80th

4. 90th   19th   **8.** 16th   60th

D. THEY GO TOGETHER

Write the ordinal number.

1. one   _first_   **4.** fifty   _____

2. three   _____   **5.** five   _____

3. ten   _____   **6.** twenty-two   _____

E. LISTENING: *WHAT'S MY NAME?*

Listen and fill in the letters where they belong.

_F_ ___ ___ _A_ ___ ___ ___ ___ ___ ___

A. WHAT'S THE WORD?

addition	division	multiplication	subtraction

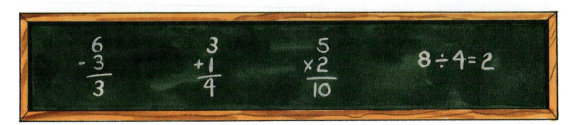

$$-\frac{6}{\frac{3}{3}} \qquad +\frac{3}{\frac{1}{4}} \qquad \times\frac{5}{\frac{2}{10}} \qquad 8 \div 4 = 2$$

1. <u>subtraction</u>   2. _____   3. _____   4. _____

B. MATCHING: WHAT'S THE SIGN?

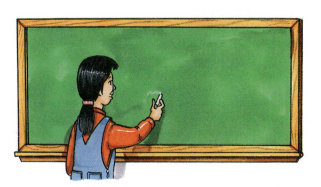

<u>b</u> **1.** plus   **a.** −

___ **2.** minus   **b.** +

___ **3.** times   **c.** =

___ **4.** divided by   **d.** x

___ **5.** equals   **e.** ÷

C. MATH SENTENCES

Write true sentences with these words. Then say the sentences.

6	plus minus times divided by	2	equals	3 4 8 12

1. _____ 6 plus 2 equals 8. _____   3. _____

2. _____   4. _____

D. WHAT'S THE PROBLEM?

Write the math problems for these sentences.

$$\frac{\begin{array}{r} 5 \\ -2 \end{array}}{3}$$

_____   _____   _____   _____

1. Five minus two equals three.   **2.** Seven plus two equals nine.   **3.** Six times two equals twelve.   **4.** Twelve divided by three is four.

31

🔊 E. LISTENING

Listen and write the number under the correct math problem.

$$-\dfrac{3}{3}\overline{}\;\;0$$ $$+\dfrac{3}{3}\overline{}\;\;6$$ $$\times\dfrac{3}{3}\overline{}\;\;9$$ $$3 \div 3 = 1$$

_____   _____   __1__   _____

F. MATCHING

<u>d</u> **1.** one quarter   **a.** 1/2

___ **2.** one third   **b.** 1/3

___ **3.** one half   **c.** 3/4

___ **4.** two thirds   **d.** 1/4

___ **5.** three fourths   **e.** 2/3

___ **6.** twenty-five percent   **f.** 50%

___ **7.** fifty percent   **g.** 100%

___ **8.** seventy-five percent   **h.** 25%

___ **9.** one hundred percent   **i.** 75%

🔊 G. LISTENING: *WHAT'S THE FRACTION?*

Listen and write the number under the correct fraction.

1/4   1/3   1/2    2/3   3/4

_____   __1__   _____   _____   _____

🔊 H. LISTENING: *WHAT'S THE PERCENT?*

Listen and write the number under the correct percent.

25%   50%    75%   100%

_____   _____   __1__   _____

32

A. WHAT TIME IS IT?

Draw the correct time on the clocks.

1. three o'clock   **2.** six fifteen   **3.** eight thirty   **4.** three forty-five

5. midnight   **6.** five oh five   **7.** a quarter after two   **8.** a quarter to ten

B. WHICH TIMES ARE CORRECT?

Circle the correct times.

1. **a.** It's four thirteen.
    b. It's four thirty.
    c. It's half past four.

2. **a.** It's two fifteen.
    b. It's a quarter to two.
    c. It's a quarter after two.

3. **a.** It's ten twenty.
    b. It's ten oh four.
    c. It's twenty after ten.

4. **a.** It's twelve forty-five.
    b. It's twelve fifty-five.
    c. It's five to one.

5. **a.** It's eight o'clock.
    b. It's eight A.M.
    c. It's eight P.M.

6. **a.** It's three forty-five.
    b. It's a quarter to three.
    c. It's a quarter to four.

C. LISTENING: *WHICH CLOCK?*

Listen and write the number under the correct clock.

_____   _____   _____   1   _____   _____

A. OUT OF ORDER: *MONTHS*

Put the months in order.

___ October
_1_ January
___ September
___ July
___ November
___ June
___ February
___ April
___ March
___ December
___ August
___ May

B. OUT OF ORDER: *DAYS*

Put the days in order.

___ Wednesday
___ Saturday
___ Monday
___ Friday
_1_ Sunday
___ Thursday
___ Tuesday

C. MATCHING

_c_ **1.** day   **a.** February
___ **2.** month   **b.** 1999
___ **3.** year   **c.** Thursday
___ **4.** date   **d.** February 28, 1999

D. LISTENING

Listen and circle the word you hear.

1. (Sunday)   Monday   **4.** September   December

2. Tuesday   Thursday   **5.** Monday   May

3. June   July   **6.** January   February

E. WRITE ABOUT TODAY

1. What day is it?   It's . . . .

2. What month is it?   It's . . . .

3. What year is it?   It's . . . .

4. What's today's date?   It's . . . .

A. MATCHING: *ASSOCIATIONS*

_c_ **1.** barber shop   **a.** dictionary
___ **2.** bank   **b.** bread
___ **3.** bakery   **c.** hair
___ **4.** book store   **d.** money

___ **5.** cleaners   **e.** doctor
___ **6.** day-care center **f.** children
___ **7.** cafeteria   **g.** lunch
___ **8.** clinic   **h.** clothes

B. A BUSY DAY

bakery	barber shop	bus station	child-care center	clinic
bank	book store	cafeteria	cleaners	convenience store

I'm going to be very busy tomorrow. First, I'm going to get some money
at the _____bank_____ [1]. Then I'm going to take my son to the
_____ [2], where he can play with his friends.
After that, I'm going to take my dirty clothes to the _____ [3].
Then I'm going to the _____ [4] for a haircut.
At 10:00 I have a doctor's appointment at the
_____ [5] in Westville. I'm going to wait for the
Westville bus at the _____ [6].
After my doctor's appointment, I'm going to have
lunch at the _____ [7] downtown.
After lunch, I'm going to buy an English dictionary
at the _____ [8]. Then I'm going to take
the bus back home. Before I get home, I'm going to buy
some bread at the _____ [9] and some milk at the _____ [10].

C. LISTENING: *WHERE ARE THEY?*

Listen and circle the correct place.

1. (bus station)   book store   **4.** bakery   bank
2. cafeteria   clinic   **5.** cleaners   day-care center
3. coffee shop   cleaners   **6.** barber shop   convenience store

A. WHICH WORD?

1. I exercise every day at the (drug store   (health club)).
2. I'm going to buy flowers at the (florist   gas station).
3. I'm going to the (hair salon   pharmacy) to get a haircut.
4. I like to stay in a (hospital   hotel) when I go on vacation.
5. You can buy medicine at the (drug store   health club).
6. I want to buy some bread at the (flower shop   grocery store).
7. You can buy gas for your car at the (drug store   service station).
8. When your leg is broken, you should go to the (hospital   health club).
9. I'm going to buy a new shirt and tie at the (department   grocery) store.
10. She's going to buy a hammer and nails at the (hair salon   hardware store).

B. LISTENING: *WHERE DID MARIA GO?*

Listen and write the number under the correct place.

___

___

___

___

___

1

___

___

A. MATCHING: *COMPLETE THE SENTENCE*

_b_ **1.** You can buy ice cream   **a.** at the music store.

___ **2.** You can buy a cat or a dog   **b.** at the ice cream shop.

___ **3.** You can wash your clothes   **c.** at the library.

___ **4.** You can look at paintings   **d.** at the motel.

___ **5.** You can buy CDs   **e.** at the museum.

___ **6.** You can get books   **f.** at the laundromat.

___ **7.** You can sleep all night   **g.** at the pet shop.

B. A WEEKEND VACATION

ice cream shop	motel	museum	park	pizza shop
library	movie theater	music store	pet shop	

Mr. and Mrs. Montero were on vacation in Brownsville last weekend. They stayed in a large room in a nice _____motel_____ [1]. On Saturday they looked at paintings in the art _____ [2]. Then they ate lunch at the _____ [3], and they had dessert at the _____ [4]. It was a beautiful day, so they sat in the _____ [5] and watched the birds. After that, Mr. Montero bought some CDs at the _____ [6], and Mrs. Montero looked at the books in the _____ [7]. They met in front of the _____ [8] and looked at the animals in the window. In the evening, they saw a film at the _____ [9]. It rained on Sunday, so they left Brownsville early and went back home.

C. LISTENING: *WHERE ARE THEY?*

Listen and circle the correct place.

1. music store   (ice cream shop)   **4.** pizza shop   parking lot

2. pet shop   pizza shop   **5.** park   museum

3. museum   movie theater   **6.** laundromat   parking garage

A. WHICH WORD?

1. You can buy a toy train at the (train station **(toy store)**).

2. I'm going to mail a letter at the (school   post office).

3. We're going to see a play at the (theater   video store).

4. Mrs. Chang is a teacher at our (school   train station).

5. We need some food. Please go to the (zoo   supermarket).

6. We're going to eat dinner at the (supermarket   restaurant).

7. You can see many different animals at the (shoe store   zoo).

8. There are many different stores in the (shopping mall   school).

9. Let's watch a movie at home tonight. I'll go to the (video store   theater).

B. CROSSWORD

ACROSS

1.
4.   7.
5.   9.

DOWN

      1.   2.   3.      6.      8.

A. WHICH GROUP?

bus	cab	courthouse	jail	police station	taxi
bus driver	cab driver	ice cream truck	meter maid	subway	taxi driver

People:

- _____bus driver_____
- _____
- _____
- _____

Places:

- _____courthouse_____
- _____
- _____

Transportation:

- _____bus_____
- _____
- _____
- _____
- _____

B. YES OR NO?

Look at page 64 of the Basic Picture Dictionary. Answer *Yes* or *No*.

__No__ **1.** The cab driver is sitting on the bench.

_____ **2.** There's a bus stop in front of the police station.

_____ **3.** The meter maid is in the subway station.

_____ **4.** The trash container is in front of the courthouse.

_____ **5.** The ice cream truck is in front of the bus.

_____ **6.** The jail is behind the police station.

_____ **7.** There are two taxis on the street.

C. WHICH WORDS ARE CORRECT?

Look at page 64 of the Basic Picture Dictionary. Circle the correct words.

1. The
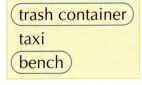
(trash container) / taxi / (bench) is on the sidewalk.

2. The bus / jail / cab is on the street.

3. The parking meter / subway / subway station is under the street.

4. The bus stop / meter maid / trash container is in front of the police station.

5. The police station / bench / subway station is next to the courthouse.

6. The subway / street light / parking meter is next to the curb.

A. WHICH WORD?

Look at page 66 of the Basic Picture Dictionary. Choose the correct word.

1. A police officer is standing in the (crosswalk (intersection)).
2. A taxi is waiting at the (taxi stand   traffic light).
3. There's a (fire alarm box   phone booth) next to the fire station.
4. A street vendor is standing next to the (traffic light   street sign).
5. The (fire station   office building) is on Main Street.
6. A garbage truck is next to the (taxi stand   newstand).
7. A (police officer   pedestrian) is crossing the street.

B. YES OR NO?

Look at page 66 of the Basic Picture Dictionary. Answer *Yes* or *No*.

Yes 1. The taxi is next to the phone booth.

_____ 2. There's a garbage truck in the fire station.

_____ 3. The fire alarm box is in front of the fire station.

_____ 4. There's a car at the drive-through window.

_____ 5. A man is standing next to the street sign.

_____ 6. Two pedestrians are crossing Main Street.

_____ 7. The street vendor is behind the newsstand.

_____ 8. Four pedestrians are using the crosswalks.

C. FIND THE PEOPLE

Where are the people on page 66 of the Basic Picture Dictionary? Write sentences that tell where the people are. Read your sentences to a friend. Ask your friend to find the people.

1. He's standing in the street between the garbage truck and the traffic light.
2. ....
3. ....
4. ....
5. ....
6. ....

A. MATCHING: *OPPOSITES*

<u>d</u> **1.** tall   **a.** tight
___ **2.** heavy   **b.** slow
___ **3.** loose   **c.** thin
___ **4.** fast   **d.** short

___ **5.** straight   **e.** little
___ **6.** good   **f.** thin
___ **7.** thick   **g.** curly
___ **8.** big   **h.** bad

___ **9.** high   **i.** old
___ **10.** wide   **j.** low
___ **11.** hot   **k.** cold
___ **12.** young   **l.** narrow

___ **13.** large   **m.** straight
___ **14.** crooked   **n.** light
___ **15.** long   **o.** small
___ **16.** dark   **p.** short

B. LISTENING: *WHAT'S THE ANSWER?*

Listen and choose the correct answer.

1. a. No. He's short.
    b. No. He's big.
2. a. No. It's curly.
    b. No. It's long.

3. a. No. It's hot.
    b. No. It's new.
4. a. No. They're dark.
    b. No. They're loose.

5. a. No. It's fast.
    b. No. It's high.
6. a. No. It's heavy.
    b. No. It's narrow.

C. WHICH WORD?

1. This box isn't light. It's (tight **(heavy)**).
2. This coat isn't short. It's (long tall).
3. My car isn't old. It's (new young).
4. My hair isn't straight. It's (light curly).
5. Our street isn't wide. It's (thin narrow).
6. The room isn't light. It's (dark heavy).
7. Our old car isn't fast. It's (low slow).
8. Her hair isn't long. It's (short small).
9. These pants aren't loose. They're (skinny tight).
10. Our dog isn't little. It's (small big).
11. My brother isn't short. He's (long tall).
12. This food isn't bad. It's (good cold).
13. This path isn't crooked. It's (straight wide).
14. That line isn't thick. It's (fat thin).

A. MATCHING: *OPPOSITES*

_b_ **1.** noisy   **a.** ugly
___ **2.** clean   **b.** quiet
___ **3.** full   **c.** empty
___ **4.** handsome **d.** dirty

___ **5.** open   **e.** hard
___ **6.** wealthy   **f.** single
___ **7.** married   **g.** poor
___ **8.** easy   **h.** closed

___ **9.** soft   **i.** cheap
___ **10.** pretty   **j.** hard
___ **11.** expensive **k.** ugly
___ **12.** shiny   **l.** dull

___ **13.** smooth   **m.** messy
___ **14.** neat   **n.** rough
___ **15.** wet   **o.** dull
___ **16.** sharp   **p.** dry

B. WHAT'S THE ANSWER?

1. Is the pitcher full?   No. It's (pretty (empty)).
2. Is the car cheap?   No. It's (rich   expensive).
3. Is the floor dull?   No. It's (shiny   sharp).
4. Is your desk neat?   No. It's (messy   smooth).
5. Is the door closed?   No. It's (empty   open).
6. Is that bed soft?   No. It's (hard   rough).
7. Are your neighbors quiet?   No. They're (loud   wealthy).
8. Is English difficult?   No. I think it's very (soft   easy).

C. LISTENING: *WHICH ONE?*

Listen and write the number under the correct picture.

_____   ___1___   _____

_____   _____   _____

A. LISTENING: *HOW DO THEY FEEL?*

Listen and choose the correct picture.

1.  ____    ✓

2.  ____    ____

3.  ____    ____

4.  ____    ____

5.  ____    ____

6.  ____    ____

7.  ____    ____

8.  ____    ____

B. HOW DO YOU FEEL TODAY?

Check the words that show how YOU feel today.

____ annoyed	____ full	____ hungry	____ thirsty
____ cold	____ happy	____ sad	____ tired
____ disappointed	____ hot	____ sick	____ upset

A. CROSSWORD

ACROSS

1.

8.

3.

9.

5.

11.

7.

12.

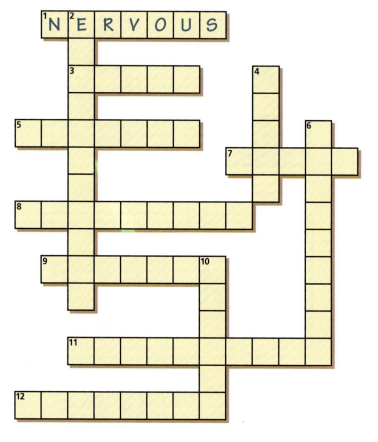

DOWN

2.

4.

6.

10.

B. HOW DO YOU FEEL WHEN . . . ?

Use words from pages 73 and 75 of the Basic Picture Dictionary to tell how YOU feel in the following situations.

1. When I eat too much, I feel . . . .

2. When I get a bad grade, I feel . . . .

3. When I get a good grade, I feel . . . .

4. When a friend doesn't listen to me, I feel . . . .
. . . .

5. When I'm very busy, I feel . . . .

6. When my homework is difficult, I feel . . . . . .
. . . .

7. When someone is angry at me, I feel . . . .

8. When I make a mistake, I feel . . . .

9. When I speak English, I feel . . . .

C. LISTENING: *HOW DO THEY FEEL?*

Listen. How do these people feel? Circle the best answer.

1. mad   (nervous)
2. embarrassed proud
3. surprised   bored
4. scared   mad
5. embarrassed angry

6. jealous   proud
7. bored   frustrated
8. surprised   mad
9. embarrassed worried
10. confused   surprised

A. WHICH FRUIT DOESN'T BELONG?

Cross out the fruit that doesn't belong.

1.
Bananas
Lemons
~~Grapes~~
Grapefruit
are yellow.

2.
Strawberries
Raisins
Raspberries
Cherries
are red.

3.
Pears
Limes
Avocadoes
Apricots
are green.

4.
Cranberries
Dates
Coconuts
Blueberries
are small.

5.
Pineapples
Honeydews
Cantaloupes
Figs
are large.

6.
Limes
Peaches
Mangoes
Nectarines
are sweet.

B. LISTENING: *WHICH FRUIT?*

Listen and check the fruit these people are talking about.

1. _____ ✔

2. _____ _____

3. _____ _____

4. _____ _____

5. _____ _____

6. _____ _____

C. FILL THE FRUIT BOWL

There is only one apple in the fruit bowl. Add your favorite fruits to the fruit bowl.
Write the names of the fruits you draw.

. . . . *apple* . . . .

. . . .

. . . .

. . . .

. . . .

A. CROSSWORD

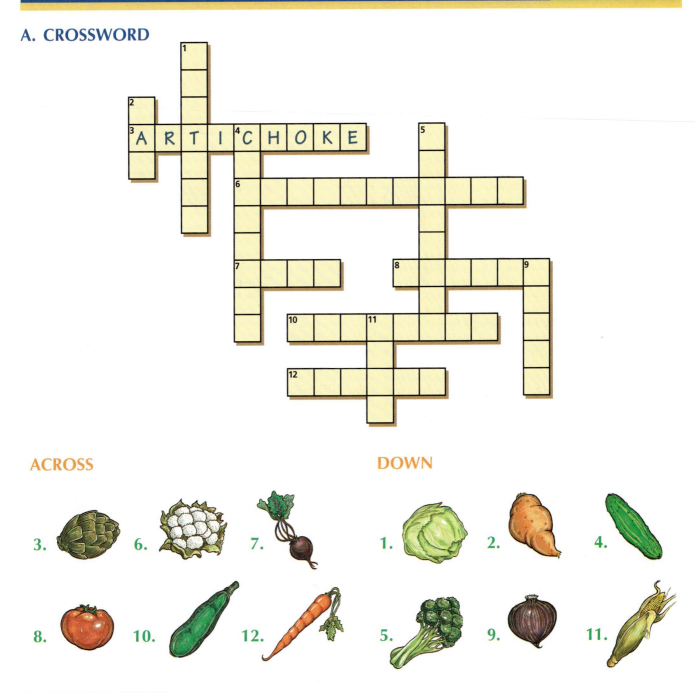

3. A R T I C H O K E

ACROSS

3. 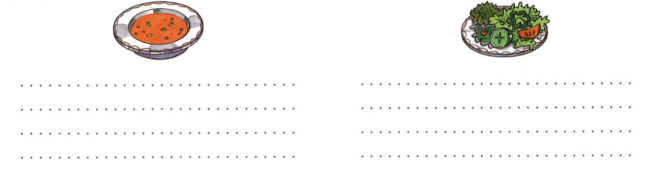 6. 7.

8. 10. 12.

DOWN

1. 2. 4.

5. 9. 11.

B. TIME TO COOK

You're going to make vegetable soup and a salad for dinner. What vegetables are you going to use?

. . . .

. . . .

. . . .

. . . .

A. MATCH THE FOODS

_e_ **1.** eggs

___ **2.** orange juice

___ **3.** milk

___ **4.** sour cream

___ **5.** yogurt

___ **6.** cheese

a.

b.

c.

d.

e.

f.

B. MATCHING: *WHERE IS IT?*

Look at page 80 of the Basic Picture Dictionary. Complete the sentences.

_b_ **1.** The milk is next to

___ **2.** The eggs are next to

___ **3.** The cream cheese is next to

___ **4.** The cheese is next to

___ **5.** The orange juice is next to

___ **6.** The yogurt is next to

a. the sour cream.

b. the chocolate milk.

c. the cottage cheese.

d. the yogurt.

e. the butter.

f. the cream.

C. WHICH WORDS ARE CORRECT?

Circle the correct words.

1. I'm eating   (cream cheese) chocolate milk (cottage cheese) .

2. Put some   cream milk sour cream   in your coffee.

3. Put some   orange juice margarine butter   on the bread.

4. I like to drink   milk orange juice yogurt .

5. I like   cheese cream egg   sandwiches.

6. I like to eat   cream cottage sour   cheese.

A. MATCH THE FOODS

<u>e</u> **1.** soap

___ **2.** spaghetti

___ **3.** crackers

___ **4.** ice cream

___ **5.** bread

___ **6.** sugar

___ **7.** cereal

___ **8.** mayonnaise

___ **9.** vinegar

___ **10.** soy sauce

___ **11.** napkins

a.

b.

c.

d.

e.

f.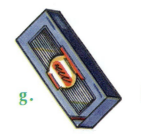

g.

h.

i.

j.

k.

B. WHERE ARE THEY?

Look at page 82 of the Basic Picture Dictionary. Choose the correct answer.

Top Shelf:

1. The soup is in front of the (crackers (cereal)).

2. The juice is next to the (soda   sugar).

3. The crackers are in front of the (spaghetti   rolls).

4. The rice is next to the (cereal   coffee).

5. The ice cream is in front of the (spaghetti   rolls).

Bottom Shelf:

6. The mayonnaise is next to the (ketchup   napkins).

7. The salad dressing is in front of the (flour   paper towels).

8. The oil is next to the (mustard   vinegar).

9. The paper towels are in front of the (pepper   toilet paper).

C. WHICH WORD DOESN'T BELONG?

Circle the word that doesn't belong.

1.	coffee	(soy sauce)	soda	tea
2.	ice cream	cake	coffee	cookies
3.	salt	pepper	spices	cereal
4.	rice	tissues	noodles	spaghetti
5.	soap	napkins	toilet paper	paper napkins
6.	bread	soup	crackers	rolls
7.	mayonnaise	sugar	ketchup	mustard
8.	oil	vinegar	salad dressing	flour

D. WHAT CAN THEY USE?

These people don't have the groceries they need. What can they use instead?

1. We don't have any spaghetti.
   How about (napkins (noodles))?

2. We don't have any ketchup.
   How about (mustard   flour)?

3. We don't have any coffee.
   How about (salad dressing   tea)?

4. We don't have any soda.
   How about (soy sauce   juice)?

5. We don't have any bread.
   How about (rolls   tissues)?

6. We don't have any salt.
   How about (soap   pepper)?

7. We don't have any cake.
   How about (cookies   vinegar)?

A. CROSSWORD

ACROSS

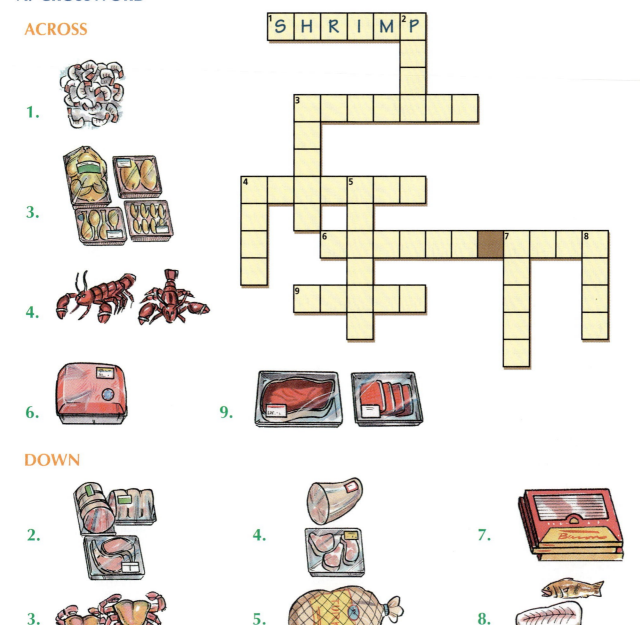

1.

3.

4.

6.

9.

DOWN

2.

3.

4.

5.

7.

8.

🎞 B. LISTENING: *THE BEST RESPONSE*

Listen and choose the best response.

1. **a.** How about some fish?
   b. How about some pork?

2. **a.** No, thanks. I don't like meat.
   b. No, thanks. I don't like seafood.

3. **a.** No, thanks. I don't eat pork.
   b. No, thanks. I don't eat poultry.

4. **a.** Let's cook some lamb.
   b. Let's cook some lobster.

5. **a.** Yes. We're having steak.
   b. Yes. We're having shrimp.

6. **a.** Okay. Here's the ham.
   b. Okay. Here's the ground beef.

A. AT THE SUPERMARKET

Look at page 86 of the Basic Picture Dictionary. Complete the sentences.

bagger	cash register	checkout line	paper bag	shopping basket
cashier	checkout counter	customer	scale	shopping cart

Asako is buying a lot of groceries today. Her son is sitting in her ___shopping cart___ **1**.
A _____ **2** is standing in front of her. He's putting his groceries on the
_____ **3**. The cashier is ringing up the prices on the _____ **4**.
She's also weighing some fruit on the _____ **5**. The _____ **6**
is helping the cashier. He's putting the groceries in a _____ **7**. There are
two shoppers in the express _____ **8**. One shopper is giving money to
the _____ **9**. The other is reading. His _____ **10** is on the
checkout counter.

B. OUT OF ORDER!

You're going shopping at the supermarket. Put the actions in the correct order.

___ Pay the cashier.

___ Walk up and down the aisles.

___ Put your groceries in your shopping basket.

___ Take your bag of groceries from the packer.

_1_ Get a shopping basket.

___ Stand in the express checkout line.

___ Put your groceries on the checkout counter.

C. WHICH WORDS ARE CORRECT?

Circle the correct words.

1. paper | (bag) / bagger

2. checkout | (line) / (counter) / customer

3. shopper / shopping | bag

4. paper / packer / plastic | bag

5. cash / cashier | register

6. shopping | counter / cart / basket

CONTAINERS AND QUANTITIES 1

A. MATCHING: *THEY GO TOGETHER*

_f_ **1.** a bunch of

___ **2.** a bottle of

___ **3.** a can of

___ **4.** a bar of

___ **5.** a bag of

___ **6.** a container of

___ **7.** a dozen

a. ketchup

b. soap

c. eggs

d. flour

e. cottage cheese

f. grapes

g. soup

B. CROSSWORD

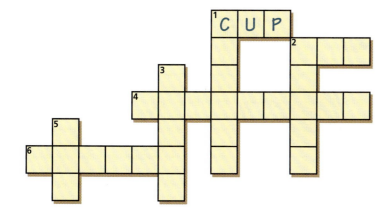

ACROSS

1. a _____ of coffee

2. a _____ of flour

4. a _____ of yogurt

6. a _____ of oil

DOWN

1. a _____ of milk

2. a _____ of bananas

3. a _____ eggs

5. a _____ of crackers

C. LISTENING: *FINISH THE SENTENCE*

Listen and circle the correct answer.

1. eggs   (salad dressing)

2. carrots   soap

3. potatoes   soup

4. ketchup   orange juice

5. coffee   eggs

6. oil   cereal

A. CROSSWORD

ACROSS

1.    3.   4.   7.   8.

DOWN

1.    2.    5.    6.

B. WHICH WORD?

TODAY'S SHOPPING LIST

1. a ((loaf)   liter) of bread
2. a (jar   pint) of ice cream
3. a (package   gallon) of rolls
4. a (quart   pound) of butter
5. six (rolls   liters) of toilet paper
6. a (pound   pint) of meat
7. three (liters   loaves) of soda
8. a (roll   jar) of mustard

C. LISTENING: *WHAT ARE THEY TALKING ABOUT?*

Listen and circle the correct answer.

1. (milk)   bread   3. butter   mayonnaise   5. potatoes   orange juice
2. bread   rolls   4. meat   ice cream   6. water   paper towels

A. WHICH WORD?

1. Put some oil in the pan. It's time to (steam (saute)) the vegetables.
2. Where's the knife? I'm going to (beat   chop) the onions.
3. I'd like a sandwich. Please (slice   stir) the bread.
4. (Mix   Scramble) the fruit and sugar together.
5. I'm going to (grate   bake) some cookies.
6. I'm going to (broil   boil) some water.
7. Please (peel   pour) the carrots.

B. WHICH WORD DOESN'T BELONG?

Circle the word that doesn't belong.

1. boil	broil	bake	(beat)
2. fry	grate	grill	saute
3. cut	chop	pour	slice
4. peel	microwave	barbecue	stir-fry
5. mix	stir	beat	cook

C. OUT OF ORDER!

Put the actions in order.

___ Stir the eggs and milk.
_1_ Put some eggs and milk in a bowl.
___ Scramble the eggs.
___ Pour the eggs and milk in a pan.

___ Chop up the onions.
___ Saute the onions.
___ Pour some oil into a pan.
_1_ Peel some onions.

1.

2.

D. HOW DO YOU COOK IT?

Tell how YOU cook these foods. Compare answers with a friend.

| bake | boil | broil | fry | grill | microwave | saute | scramble | steam | stir-fry |

1. eggs . . . .
2. chicken . . . .
3. vegetables . . . .
4. potatoes . . . .
5. fish . . . .
6. your favorite food . . . .

A. FIX THE MENU!

Some letters are missing from the menu. Fill in the missing letters.

1. d _o_ _n_ _u_ t

2. b __ g __ __

3. __ __ f f __ __

4. __ __ f f __ __

5. p __ __ __ __ y

6. __ __ z z __

7. __ __ m __ n __ __ __

8. __ __ __ __ d __ g

9. i __ __ __ __ t __ __

B. WHAT SHOULD THEY ORDER?

1. I'd like something to drink. How about a ((soda) bagel)?
2. I'd like something to eat. How about a (decaf coffee biscuit)?
3. What can I have for breakfast? How about a (muffin cheeseburger)?
4. I'd like a cold drink. How about some (tea iced tea)?
5. I'd like something sweet. How about a (donut taco)?

C. WHICH WORD DOESN'T BELONG?

Circle the word that doesn't belong.

1. (muffin) hamburger hot dog sandwich
2. tea coffee biscuit soda
3. biscuit pastry donut milk
4. iced tea milk lemonade coffee
5. donut taco muffin bagel

A. MATCHING: *WHAT DO THEY DO?*

_c_ **1.** A dishwasher   **a.** cleans tables.

___ **2.** A cook   **b.** takes money.

___ **3.** A busboy   **c.** washes dishes.

___ **4.** A waiter   **d.** prepares food.

___ **5.** A cashier   **e.** brings food.

B. AT THE RESTAURANT

Look at page 96 of the Basic Picture Dictionary. Complete the sentences.

booster seat	busboy	dishwasher	menu	waiter
booth	cashier	high chair	table	waitress

Mr. and Mrs. Roberts are sitting at a _____table_____ [1] with their daughter Julie.

Mr. and Mrs. Roberts are reading the _____ [2]. Julie is sitting in a

_____ [3]. Two men are sitting in a _____ [4] near the

window. A _____ [5] is bringing food. A _____ [6] is

cleaning a table. There's a _____ [7] in the booth. A man and a

woman are sitting near the cashier. The woman is talking to the _____ [8].

The _____ [9] is putting money in the cash register. Two people are

working in the kitchen — the cook and the _____ [10].

🔈 C. LISTENING: *YES OR NO?*

Look at page 96 of the Basic Picture Dictionary. Listen to the questions about the picture
and answer *Yes* or *No*.

1. Yes   (No)   **3.** Yes   No   **5.** Yes   No   **7.** Yes   No

2. Yes   No   **4.** Yes   No   **6.** Yes   No   **8.** Yes   No

A. WHAT'S THE COLOR?

<u>blue</u>	_____	_____	_____	_____
ocean	milk	STOP	banana	GO
sky	teeth	apple	butter	grass
jeans	chalk	tomato	lemon	dollar

B. MIX THE COLORS

beige	gray	green	orange	pink	purple

1. blue + yellow = _____*green*_____
2. red + yellow = _____
3. red + white = _____

4. black + white = _____
5. brown + white = _____
6. blue + red = _____

C. LISTENING: *FAVORITE COLORS*

Listen and check these people's favorite colors.

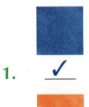

1. ✓ ____   4. ____ ____

2. ____ ____   5. ____ ____

3. ____ ____   6. ____ ____

D. YOUR COLORS

Complete these sentences about YOURSELF using colors.

1. My eyes are . . . .
2. My bedroom is . . . .
3. My classroom is . . . .
4. My English book is . . . .

5. My notebook is . . . .
6. My favorite fruit is . . . .
7. My favorite flower is . . . .
8. My country's flag is . . . .

A. WHICH WORD?

1. When I play tennis I usually wear (a sports jacket (shorts)).

2. It's cold today. Put on your (tie   sweater).

3. Peter is wearing a (skirt   shirt) under his sweater.

4. A woman's suit is a skirt and a (jacket   blouse).

5. It's hot today. I'm going to wear my (shorts   suit).

6. David is wearing jeans and (slacks   a shirt).

7. Nina is wearing a skirt and a (blouse   dress).

8. Alfred is wearing a suit and (pants   a tie).

B. LISTENING: *WHAT ARE THEY TALKING ABOUT?*

Listen and circle the clothing item you hear.

1. (suit)   skirt   4. skirt   shirt

2. shorts   sports jacket   5. jacket   slacks

3. vest   dress   6. shirts   shorts

C. WHAT SHOULD THEY WEAR?

Help these people decide what to wear.

a blouse	jeans	a shirt	a skirt	a sports jacket	a sweater	a uniform
a dress	pants	shorts	slacks	a suit	a tie	a vest

1. I'm going to a job interview.   Wear . . . .

2. This is my first day in my new school.   Wear . . . .

3. I'm going to a very nice restaurant.   Wear . . . .

4. I'm going to clean the garage today.   Wear . . . .

5. I'm going on vacation in YOUR   Wear . . . .

A. WHICH GROUP?

boots	bra	nightgown	panties	shoes	sneakers	undershirt
boxer shorts	briefs	pajamas	sandals	slip	underpants	

Men's underwear:
- _____briefs_____
- _____
- _____
- _____

Women's underwear:
- _____
- _____
- _____

Sleepwear:
- _____
- _____

Footwear:
- _____
- _____
- _____
- _____

B. WHICH WORD?

1. You wear pajamas or a (bathrobe (nightgown)) when you sleep.
2. You wear (boots   sandals) when it's cold.
3. You wear (slippers   sneakers) when you play tennis.
4. You wear boxer (shoes   shorts) under jeans or slacks.
5. You wear (a bra   briefs) under a blouse.
6. You wear (boots   sandals) at the beach.
7. You wear a slip under (a dress   pants).
8. You wear (pantyhose   pajamas) under a bathrobe.
9. You wear (a slip   socks) on your feet.

C. WHICH WORD DOESN'T BELONG?

Circle the word that doesn't belong.

1. stockings   pantyhose   (pajamas)   socks
2. sneakers   slippers   slip   sandals
3. stockings   pajamas   bathrobe   nightgown
4. bra   boots   briefs   panties
5. undershirt   underpants   boxer shorts nightgown

A. WHICH GROUP?

coat	ear muffs	jacket	mittens	raincoat	running shorts	sweatshirt
down vest	gloves	jogging suit	poncho	rubbers	scarf	tee shirt

You wear these when it's cold:

- _____coat_____
- _____
- _____
- _____
- _____
- _____
- _____

You wear these when it rains:

- _____
- _____
- _____

You wear these when you exercise:

- _____
- _____
- _____
- _____

B. MATCHING: *WHERE DO THEY GO?*

_d_	1. sunglasses	a.	head
___	2. scarf	b.	ears
___	3. gloves	c.	feet
___	4. baseball cap	d.	eyes
___	5. rubbers	e.	hands
___	6. ear muffs	f.	neck

C. WHICH WORD DOESN'T BELONG?

1. running shorts   (hat)   sweat pants   jogging suit
2. mittens   scarf   swimsuit   ear muffs
3. baseball cap   coat   down vest   jacket
4. raincoat   rubbers   sunglasses   poncho

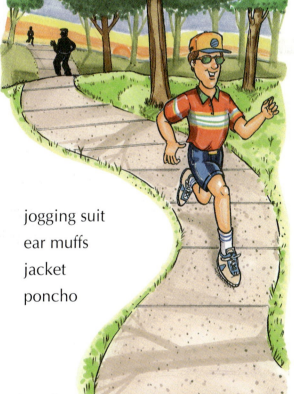

🔊 D. LISTENING: *THE BEST RESPONSE*

Listen and choose the best answer.

1. (a.) Wear your gloves.
   b. Wear your rubbers.

2. a. Wear your down vest.
   b. Wear your poncho.

3. a. Wear your swimsuit.
   b. Wear your sweat pants.

4. a. Wear your hat and scarf.
   b. Wear your sunglasses.

A. MATCHING: *THEY GO TOGETHER*

_c_ **1.** key   **a.** purse

___ **2.** cuff   **b.** bag

___ **3.** wedding   **c.** ring

___ **4.** book   **d.** band

___ **5.** change   **e.** links

B. LISTENING: *WHAT ARE THEY TALKING ABOUT?*

Listen and circle the correct word.

1. key ring   (earring)   **4.** cuff links   rings

2. belt   wallet   **5.** book bag   backpack

3. briefcase   bracelet   **6.** watch   wallet

C. WHAT'S THE WORD?

briefcase   change purse   pin   umbrella   watch

1. I'm looking for some money in my ___change purse___ .

2. It's raining outside. I need my _____.

3. Peter carries his books and papers to work in a _____.

4. I'm sorry. I don't know the time. I'm not wearing a _____.

5. Susan is wearing a beautiful diamond _____ on her blouse.

D. WHICH WORDS ARE CORRECT?

Circle the correct words.

1. You wear (a bracelet) / a wallet / (earrings) .

2. You wear a ring / wedding band / key ring on your finger.

3. You carry money in a cuff link / change purse / wallet .

4. You carry books in a book bag / pocketbook / briefcase .

5. You buy a pin / a necklace / an umbrella at the jewelry store.

6. You carry a key ring / backpack / change purse in a pocketbook.

A. WHAT'S THE WORD?

heavy	long	loose	low	plain	tight

1. Is this dress too fancy? No. I think it's too ___plain___.

2. Are these heels too high? No. I think they're too _____.

3. Is this coat too light? No. I think it's too _____.

4. Is this blouse too tight? No. I think it's too _____.

5. Is this skirt too short? No. I think it's too _____.

6. Are these pants too baggy? No. I think they're too _____.

B. WHICH WORDS ARE CORRECT?

Circle the correct words.

1. That jacket is too
   - (short)
   - (small)
   - low

2. That color is too
   - loose
   - light
   - dark

3. Those shoes are too
   - narrow
   - baggy
   - wide

4. Those heels are too
   - high
   - low
   - long

5. That blouse is too
   - plain
   - high
   - tight

6. That coat is too
   - low
   - heavy
   - big

C. LISTENING: *THE BEST ANSWER*

Listen and choose the best answer.

1. a. Yes. It's very long.
   b. Yes. It's very short.

2. a. Yes. They're very baggy.
   b. Yes. They're very narrow.

3. a. Yes. They're very loose.
   b. Yes. They're very tight.

4. a. No. The sleeves are too long.
   b. No. The heels are too high.

5. a. No. They're too long.
   b. No. They're too plain.

6. a. No. It's too wide.
   b. No. It's too dark.

A. WHAT COIN IS IT?

| dime | half dollar | nickel | penny | quarter | silver dollar |

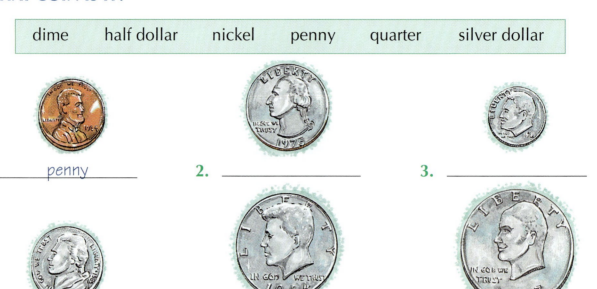

1. _____penny_____

2. _____

3. _____

4. _____

5. _____

6. _____

B. LISTENING: *HOW MUCH?*

Listen and put a check under the correct coins.

1. ✓ _____   _____

2. _____   _____

3. _____   _____

4. _____   _____

5. _____   _____

6. _____   _____

C. WHICH IS DIFFERENT?

1. penny   1¢ $ .01   ($1.00)
2. half dollar nickel   50¢   fifty cents
3. 25¢   quarter $25 $.25
4. dime $10   ten cents   10¢
5. 50¢ $.05   5¢   nickel

A. MATCHING: *WORDS AND NUMBERS*

_c_ **1.** one dollar   **a.** $10.00   ___ **4.** five dollars   **d.** $15.00

___ **2.** ten dollars   **b.** $100.00   ___ **5.** fifty dollars   **e.** $5.00

___ **3.** one hundred dollars   **c.** $1.00   ___ **6.** fifteen dollars   **f.** $50.00

B. HOW MUCH IS IT?

1. _____eleven dollars_____   **2.** _____

3. _____   **4.** _____

5. _____   **6.** _____

C. HOW MUCH MONEY DO THEY HAVE?

1. Elena has a one-hundred dollar bill and a fifty. She has _____$150.00_____.

2. George has a five-dollar bill and a dime. He has _____.

3. Peter has a twenty-dollar bill and a five. He has _____.

4. Lisa has a ten-dollar bill and a quarter. She has _____.

5. Susan has a fifty-dollar bill and a ten. She has _____.

6. Jack has 2 twenty-dollar bills. He has _____.

7. John has 2 five-dollar bills. He has _____.

D. LISTENING: *HOW MUCH?*

Listen and circle the correct amount.

1. ($25.00) $15.00   **3.** $4.25 $40.25   **5.** $3.25 $.75

2. $10.00 $.05   **4.** $.06 $6.00   **6.** $20.25 $25.20

A. WHICH WORD?

1. When you put money in your bank account, you fill out a ((deposit) withdrawal) slip.

2. I'm going to write a check. Where's my (bank book   checkbook)?

3. When you take money out of your bank account, you fill out a (money order   withdrawal slip).

4. Put your (ATM card   checkbook) in the cash machine.

5. You can pay with a check or a (bank book   credit card).

6. When you cash a check, you talk to a (bank teller   money order).

7. When you open a bank account, you talk to a (security guard   bank officer).

8. When the bank is closed, you can get money from the (ATM machine   teller).

B. WHAT ARE THEY SAYING?

bank manager	check	vault	withdrawal slip

1. **A.** I want to open a bank account.
   B. Talk to the ____bank manager____.

2. **A.** May I help you?
   B. Yes. I'd like to put these papers in the _____.

3. **A.** I'd like to cash this _____.
   B. Okay. Sign your name on the back.

4. **A.** I'd like to take some money out of my bank account.
   B. Fill out a _____.

C. WRITE A CHECK

Write a check to a company, store, or person you know. You decide the amount and what the check is for. Don't forget to write the date and sign the check.

Pay to the order of _____ $ _____

_____ Dollars

For _____ _____

42-51/409

A. WE HAVE TWO OF THESE!

Circle the parts of the body that we have two of.

chin	mouth	eyebrow	thigh
(eye)	lip	forehead	waist
nose	shoulder	face	cheek
elbow	knee	leg	hip
ear	chest	neck	tongue

B. FROM TOP TO BOTTOM!

Where do they go? Arrange the parts of the body from top to bottom.

chin eye eyebrow forehead mouth nose	abdomen chest face leg neck shoulder	back calf hip knee thigh waist

- forehead
- ___
- ___
- ___
- ___
- chin

- face
- ___
- ___
- ___
- ___
- ___

- back
- ___
- ___
- ___
- ___
- ___

C. WHICH WORD?

1. My grandfather has a long gray beard on his (shin (chin)).
2. The dentist says, "Open your (tongue   mouth)."
3. I can't wear this belt. My (jaw   waist) is too big.
4. I can't wear these pants. My (hips   lips) are too large.
5. I can't wear this shirt. My (neck   knee) and my (shoulders   shins) are too big.
6. I can't move my right (elbow   face)!
7. My daughter's (eyes   ears) are blue.
8. I can't run. I'm having a problem with my (forehead   knee).

A. YOU'RE THE DOCTOR!

1. My back hurts!   I'll X-ray your (heel (spinal cord)).

2. I have pains in my chest!   I'll listen to your (heart   liver).

3. It hurts when I talk!   I'll look at your (throat   thumb).

4. I have terrible pains after I eat!   I'll check your (lungs   stomach).

5. My hand hurts!   Can you move your (wrist   ankle)?

6. My foot hurts!   Can you move your (fingers   toes)?

B. MATCHING: *WHERE ARE THEY?*

_d_ 1.	spinal cord	a.	neck
___ 2.	throat	b.	foot
___ 3.	heart and lungs	c.	hand
___ 4.	toes	d.	back
___ 5.	stomach	e.	abdomen
___ 6.	palm	f.	head
___ 7.	brain	g.	chest

C. HOW MANY DO WE HAVE?

1.	hands	_2_	7.	thumbs	___
2.	fingers	___	8.	fingernails	___
3.	feet	___	9.	heels	___
4.	ankles	___	10.	hearts	___
5.	toes	___	11.	lungs	___
6.	wrists	___	12.	kidneys	___

D. WHICH WORD DOESN'T BELONG?

1.	hand	thumb	(foot)	finger
2.	ankle	lungs	toe	heel
3.	brain	heart	toenail	lungs
4.	stomach	large intestine	pancreas	palm
5.	skin	liver	lungs	kidneys
6.	thumb	finger	throat	toe

A. WHAT'S THE MATTER WITH THEM?

a backache	a cold	a fever	a stiff neck	a toothache
the chills	an earache	an insect bite	a sunburn	

1. I have ___a cold___ .

2. I have _____ .

3. I have _____ .

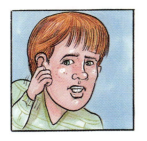

4. I have _____ .

5. I have _____ .

6. I have _____ .

7. I have _____ .

8. I have _____ .

9. I have _____ .

B. WHAT DO THEY HAVE?

Circle the correct word.

1. a sore [head / (throat)]

3. an insect [burn / bite]

5. a [cavity / cough] in my tooth

2. a [runny / rash] nose

4. a stiff [neck / nose]

6. an [earache / infection] on my arm

📼 **C. LISTENING:** *WHAT'S THE MATTER?*

Listen and choose the correct answer.

1. toothache   (headache)   3. cold   cough   5. hiccups   chills

2. sore throat   stomachache   4. virus   rash   6. runny nose   bloody nose

D. CROSSWORD

ACROSS

2.

6.

9.

11.

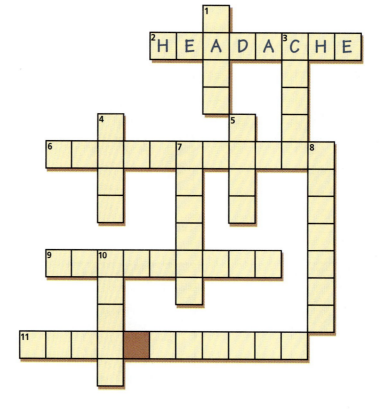

DOWN

1.   3.    4.    5.

7.   8.    10.

A. WHAT ARE THEY SAYING?

bleeding	bruised	congested	dizzy	itchy	sneeze	throw up
broke	burned	dislocated	exhausted	nauseous	swollen	

1. I think I <u>dislocated</u> my shoulder.

2. Ouch! I _____ my hand!

3. I have a bad cold. I'm very _____.

4. Ouch! I _____ my elbow!

5. Oh, no! I'm going to _____.

6. My finger is very _____.

7. I cut my finger. It's _____.

8. I feel _____. I'm going to _____.

9. Help! I think I _____ my leg.

10. I'm very _____.

11. I'm really _____!

12. My toes are _____.

B. WHICH WORD DOESN'T BELONG?

1. scrape — (sneeze) — scratch — bruise

2. coughing — wheezing — bleeding — sneezing

3. twist — burp — sprain — dislocate

4. faint — nauseous — swollen — dizzy

5. burp — vomit — throw up — cut

C. LISTENING: *WHAT'S THE MATTER?*

What's the matter? Is it a cold, a stomach virus, or an injury? Listen and circle the correct answer.

1. cold   stomach virus   (injury)
2. cold   stomach virus   injury
3. cold   stomach virus   injury
4. cold   stomach virus   injury
5. cold   stomach virus   injury

6. cold   stomach virus   injury
7. cold   stomach virus   injury
8. cold   stomach virus   injury
9. cold   stomach virus   injury
10. cold   stomach virus   injury

D. WHAT'S THE WORD?

1. My finger is ((swollen)   faint) and (dizzy   itchy). I think I have an insect bite.

2. I feel (bloated   congested) because I ate too much.

3. My finger is bleeding. I (cut   twisted) it.

4. Did you (break   sprain) a muscle?

5. I (broke   twisted) a bone.

6. I fell down and (burned   scraped) my knee.

7. I don't feel well today. I feel (nauseous   dislocated).

8. Edward is (sneezing   burping) because he drank too fast.

E. WHICH WORDS ARE CORRECT?

Circle the correct words.

1. My finger is
   - (bleeding)
   - (swollen)
   - bloated
   .

2. I
   - scraped
   - sneezed
   - scratched
   my elbow.

3. I
   - bruised
   - burned
   - burped
   my hand.

4. I
   - twisted
   - congested
   - sprained
   my ankle.

5. I
   - exhausted
   - hurt
   - broke
   my leg.

6. I have a cold. I'm
   - congested
   - sneezing
   - bloated
   .

MEDICAL AND DENTAL CARE

A. WHO SHOULD THEY CALL?

Tell these people who they should call.

> a cardiologist   a dentist   an obstetrician   an optometrist   a pediatrician   a surgeon

1. I have a toothache!   Call _____*a dentist*_____!
2. I'm having problems with my eyes!   Call _____!
3. My child is sick!   Call _____!
4. I'm having problems with my heart!   Call _____!
5. I need to have an operation!   Call _____!
6. I think I'm going to have a baby!   Call _____!

B. WHAT WILL THEY DO?

> adhesive tape   eye chart   scale   thermometer
> examination table   Novocaine   stethoscope   X-ray machine

1. The doctor will listen to your heart with a _____*stethoscope*_____.

2. The nurse will take your temperature with a _____.

3. The nurse will put some _____ on the bandage.

4. The optometrist will ask you to read the _____.

5. The dentist will give you some _____ before he drills your tooth.

6. The nurse will ask you to stand on the _____ so she can weigh you.

7. The doctor will ask you to lie down on the _____. Then she'll examine you.

8. The technician will take a picture of your lungs with the _____.

C. LISTENING: *WHO'S TALKING?*

Listen and circle the correct person.

1. psychiatrist   (X-ray technician)   5. EMT   nurse
2. hygienist   optometrist   6. optometrist   lab technician
3. cardiologist   dentist   7. psychiatrist   surgeon
4. pediatrician   gynecologist   8. pediatrician   obstetrician

A. WHICH WORD?

1. You need to drink ((fluids)   gargle).
2. Put this (sling   bandaid) on your finger.
3. Please put on this hospital (bed   gown).
4. You'll have to wear a (cast   sling) on your leg.
5. After surgery, you'll have to walk with (crutches   exercise).
6. After the operation, you'll get fluids from an (I.V.   injection).
7. Press the (bed control   call button) when you need a nurse.
8. The nurse gave me (an injection   X-rays) in my arm.
9. Don't exercise for a few days. You need to (gargle   rest) in bed.
10. I can't eat sugar, salt, or butter. I don't like this (physical therapy   diet).
11. The doctor is writing a (medical chart   prescription) for my new medicine.
12. When you need to go to the bathroom, you can use this (bed pan   bed table).

B. IN THE HOSPITAL

bed control	crutches	hospital gown	I.V.	tests
call button	fluids	injection	rest	therapy

This is your room in the hospital. Here's your bed. You can move your bed up and down with the ___bed control___ [1]. Press the _____ [2] when you need a nurse. You can wear this _____ [3]. You're going to have surgery in the afternoon. In the morning, you'll need to have some blood _____ [4]. Don't worry about the surgery. The doctor will give you an _____ [5] and you'll go to sleep. When you wake up, you'll be fine. You'll have to _____ [6] in bed for a few days, and you'll have to drink _____ [7]. You'll also get fluids from an _____ [8]. After a few days, you'll get physical _____ [9]. You'll learn how to walk with _____ [10]. At the end of the week, you'll go home.

A. MATCHING: *WHAT DO I NEED?*

_d_ **1.** I have a sore throat.

___ **2.** I have a stomachache.

___ **3.** I have a cough.

___ **4.** I have a cold.

___ **5.** I have a headache.

___ **6.** I have a burn.

a. You need decongestant spray.

b. You need ointment.

c. You need aspirin.

d. You need throat lozenges.

e. You need cough syrup.

f. You need antacid tablets.

B. WHICH WORD DOESN'T BELONG?

1. capsule   pill   (teaspoon)   tablet

2. creme   decongestant   lotion   ointment

3. cold tablets   cough syrup   throat lozenges   tablespoon

4. aspirin   cold tablets   ice pack   vitamins

C. LISTENING: *WHAT'S THE WORD?*

Listen and circle the word you hear.

1. (capsules)   caplets   **3.** lozenges   lotion   **5.** teaspoon   tablespoon

2. spray   syrup   **4.** tablet   caplet   **6.** pack   pad

D. WHICH WORDS ARE CORRECT?

Circle the correct words.

1. (cold) / (antacid) / eye   tablets

2. cough   spray / drops / syrup

3. eye / cough / throat   drops

4. aspirin   lotion / tablets / caplets

5. decongestant / antacid / nasal   spray

6. skin   lotion / lozenge / creme

E. TELL ABOUT YOURSELF

What do YOU do when you're sick? Do you take or use medicine? Do you do something else?

When I have a cold, I . . . .

When I have a stomachache, I . . . .

When I have a . . . . , I . . . .

THE POST OFFICE

A. MATCHING: *FINISH THE WORDS*

_c_	**1.** book	**a.** class		___	**4.** parcel	**d.** code
___	**2.** first	**b.** mail		___	**5.** letter	**e.** post
___	**3.** air	**c.** rate		___	**6.** zip	**f.** carrier

B. WHICH WORD?

1. The letter carrier drives (an express mail ⟨a mail truck⟩).
2. Write your return address on the (aerogramme   air mail).
3. The (postal clerk   letter carrier) brings the mail.
4. I have to send money. I think I'll buy a (money order   package).
5. You can buy stamps from the (postal clerk   mailbox).
6. They need this tomorrow. I'm going to send it (registered   express) mail.
7. This letter is for Luis. Write his (address   return address) on the envelope.
8. We're moving. We have to fill out a (parcel post   change-of-address) form.

C. WHICH WORDS ARE CORRECT?

Circle the correct words.

1. I need   ⟨a roll⟩ / an order / ⟨a sheet⟩   of stamps.

2. Send it   air mail / first class / return address   .

3. Put a stamp on the   envelope / parcel post / postcard   .

4. What's your   address / stamp / zip code   ?

5. I have to mail   a book rate / a package / an aerogramme   .

6. She's a postal   carrier / clerk / worker   .

7. Send it   express / parcel / registered   mail.

8. I'm buying a   stamp / money order / mailbox   .

A. WHAT ARE THEY SAYING?

1. **A.** Where are the magazines?

   B. They're over there on the ((shelves)   checkout desk).

2. **A.** I want to take out this book.

   B. Where's your (call   library) card?

3. **A.** Where can I find a map of the United States?

   B. Look in the (dictionary   atlas).

4. **A.** Where can I find "Plants of North America" by William Fitch?

   B. Look in the (card catalog   encyclopedia).

5. **A.** I can't find a book.

   B. Ask the (call card   librarian) at the information desk for help.

6. **A.** Excuse me. Do you have today's (newspaper   library assistant)?

   B. Yes. It's over there.

7. **A.** I don't understand that word.

   B. Look in the (newspaper   dictionary).

B. WHICH WORDS ARE CORRECT?

Circle the correct words.

1. library   (card) (assistant) encyclopedia

2. dictionary information checkout desk

3. call catalog library card

C. OUT OF ORDER!

You're taking a book out of the library. Put the actions in order.

___ Go to the shelves.

___ Go to the checkout desk.

___ Take the book home.

___ Find the call card.

_1_ Look in the card catalog.

___ Give the librarian your library card.

___ Find the book.

A. WHICH WORD?

1. Carmen is sick. She's going to see the (assistant principal (school nurse)).
2. I'm going to talk to the (custodian   guidance counselor) about my courses.
3. It's a beautiful day. I'm going to run around the (track   auditorium).
4. Put your books in your (lounge   locker).
5. The (coach   custodian) cleans our school.
6. The students are playing football in the (field   bleachers).
7. The (coach   driver's ed instructor) teaches us how to drive.
8. The (principal   custodian) is the head of the school.

B. WHERE ARE THEY?

auditorium	cafeteria	classroom	language lab
bleachers	chemistry lab	gym	locker room

1. Richard is listening to English language tapes. He's in the _____language lab_____.
2. The 10th grade students are watching a movie. They're in the _____.
3. Ruth and her classmates are eating lunch. They're in the _____.
4. Carol is doing chemistry experiments. She's in the _____.
5. My friends and I are watching a football game outside. We're in the _____.
6. Jeff is putting on his gym clothes. He's in the _____.
7. Ron and Howard are playing volleyball inside. They're in the _____.
8. Mrs. Wong is teaching a mathematics class. She's in her _____.

C. LISTENING: WHO'S TALKING?

Listen and decide who is speaking.

1. (school nurse)   custodian
2. principal   coach
3. guidance counselor   custodian
4. driver's ed instructor principal
5. custodian   teacher
6. driver's ed instructor coach

SCHOOL SUBJECTS

A. WHAT SUBJECTS SHOULD THEY STUDY?

art	geography	history		math	science
English	health	home economics		music	Spanish

1. I want to learn about the human body.

   You should study _____ health _____.

2. I want to visit Mexico.

   You should study _____.

3. I want to learn about plants.

   You should study _____.

4. I want to learn about the French revolution.

   You should study _____.

5. I want to learn how to draw.

   You should study _____.

6. I want to learn about famous composers.

   You should study _____.

7. I like numbers!

   You should study _____.

8. I like to learn about rivers and mountains.

   You should study _____.

9. I want to learn how to cook.

   You should study _____.

10. I'm going to move to the United States.

    You should study _____.

A. CROSSWORD

ACROSS

1. Alice wants to be the president of the class. She enjoys _____.
2. I play the violin in the school _____.
5. Mark writes poetry for our school _____.
7. David plays on the _____ team.
8. I sing in the school _____.

DOWN

1. I write articles for the _____.
3. Peter is an actor. He enjoys _____.
4. I play the trombone in the school _____.
6. I'm looking at the pictures in the _____.

B. LISTENING: *WHICH ACTIVITY?*

Listen and write the number next to the correct activity.

_____ band   1 choir   _____ drama   _____ football   _____ student government

A. WHAT DO THEY USE?

_d_ **1.** An artist uses   **a.** scissors.

___ **2.** An accountant uses   **b.** a cash register.

___ **3.** A butcher uses   **c.** a hammer.

___ **4.** A barber uses   **d.** a paintbrush.

___ **5.** A carpenter uses   **e.** a knife.

___ **6.** A cashier uses   **f.** a computer.

B. WHAT'S THE OCCUPATION?

accountant   actress   bricklayer   bus driver   butcher   carpenter   cashier

1. Dan is a ___bricklayer___. He builds walls and fireplaces.
2. I cut meat in a supermarket. I'm a _____.
3. Jan is learning to drive a bus. She wants to be a _____.
4. Marlene is an _____ in Hollywood. She's in a new movie.
5. Peter uses a cash register. He's a very good _____.
6. Mr. Larsen is a _____. He fixes things in our house.
7. Mrs. Ng is an _____. She helps us with our taxes.

C. LISTENING: *WHO'S TALKING?*

Listen and circle the correct job.

1. (cashier)   accountant   **4.** assembler   butcher
2. carpenter   barber   **5.** artist   carpenter
3. bus driver   bricklayer   **6.** actor   accountant

A. WHAT'S THE OCCUPATION?

| chef | electrician | farmer | fisherman | foreman | hairdresser | housekeeper |

1. My grandson Tommy likes to catch fish. He wants to be a _____fisherman_____.
2. I work in a factory. I'm a _____.
3. Pierre cooks in a restaurant. He's a _____.
4. Marie works in a hotel. She's a _____.
5. Anthony cuts women's hair. He's a _____.
6. Fred is a _____. He grows vegetables.
7. Irene fixes electrical wiring. She's an _____.

B. MATCHING: *WHAT'S THE WORD?*

Draw a line to complete the word. Then write the word on the line.

1. fisher   dresser   _____fisherman_____
2. hair   man   _____
3. house   man   _____
4. fore   keeper   _____

C. OUT OF PLACE!

Which people don't belong?

They prepare food:

1.
chef
~~electrician~~
cook

They grow things:

3.
farmer
gardener
construction worker

They work outside:

2.
hairdresser
farmer
fisherman

They clean:

4.
custodian
janitor
delivery person
housekeeper

A. CROSSWORD

ACROSS

1. I work for a newspaper. I'm a _____.
2. I paint houses. I'm a _____.
4. I help people understand the law. I'm a _____.
6. I fix pipes in people's bathrooms. I'm a _____.
8. I sell medicine in a drug store. I'm a _____.

DOWN

1. I fix refrigerators and dishwashers. I'm a _____.
3. I sell clothing in a department store. I'm a _____.
5. I carry messages to people. I'm a _____.
7. I work in a garage. I'm a _____.

B. LISTENING: *WHO'S TALKING?*

Listen and circle the correct job.

1. (mechanic)   messenger   4. reporter   repairperson
2. plumber   pharmacist   5. painter   lawyer
3. salesperson   sanitation worker 6. plumber   police officer

A. WHAT'S THE WORD?

weld	weld**er**
wait	wait**er**

1. I *weld* things. I'm a _____ welder _____ .
2. I *drive* a truck. I'm a _____ .
3. I *drive* a taxi. I'm a _____ .
4. I *report* the news. I'm a _____ .
5. I *paint* houses. I'm a _____ .
6. I *assemble* parts. I'm an _____ .
7. I *wait* on people in a restaurant. I'm a _____ .

B. WHICH WORD?

1. Bob works in an office. He's a (welder (secretary)).
2. Sally drives a cab. She's a (taxi driver   truck driver).
3. I sew clothes. I'm a very good (seamstress   waitress).
4. I work in a department store. I'm a (scientist   stock clerk).
5. Vincent works in a factory. He's a (waitress   welder).
6. Barbara works in a laboratory. She's a (scientist   seamstress).
7. I guard a large office building downtown. I'm a (security guard   scientist).
8. John works in a restaurant. He's a (waiter   waitress).
9. John's sister also works in a restaurant. She's a (waiter   waitress).
10. I always take my dog to Dr. Watson. He's a very good (stock clerk   veterinarian).

C. LISTENING: *WHO'S TALKING?*

Listen and circle the correct job.

1. (scientist)   waiter
2. welder   waitress
3. veterinarian   truck driver
4. secretary   stock clerk
5. security guard   seamstress
6. stock clerk   taxi driver

A. WHICH WORD?

1. Susan can drive a ((truck) lawn).
2. I (assemble   act) components.
3. I like to (mow   grow) vegetables.
4. David (drives   delivers) pizzas.
5. I (file   drive) in an office.
6. I like to (cook   build) furniture.
7. I can (guard   grow) buildings.
8. Can you (file   mow) lawns?
9. Do you like to (cook   construct) dinner?

B. MATCHING: *WHAT DO THEY DO?*

_c_	1. Truck drivers	a.	file.
___	2. Chefs	b.	assemble components.
___	3. Assemblers	c.	drive trucks.
___	4. Actors	d.	grow vegetables.
___	5. Farmers	e.	cook.
___	6. Secretaries	f.	act.

___	7. Delivery people	g.	build things.
___	8. Housekeepers	h.	mow lawns.
___	9. Security guards	i.	clean.
___	10. Gardeners	j.	guard buildings.
___	11. Carpenters	k.	deliver things.

C. HOW ABOUT YOU?

Look at pages 146-147 of the Basic Picture Dictionary and tell about YOURSELF.

Which work activities can you do?

I can . . . .

. . . .

Which work activities do you like to do?

I like to . . . .

. . . .

A. MATCHING: *WHAT DO THEY DO?*

_d_ **1.** Painters   **a.** fix things.

___ **2.** Repairpeople   **b.** write.

___ **3.** Salespeople   **c.** sew.

___ **4.** Seamstresses   **d.** paint.

___ **5.** Writers   **e.** sell things.

___ **6.** Singers   **f.** type.

___ **7.** Teachers   **g.** sing.

___ **8.** Pianists   **h.** serve food.

___ **9.** Waiters   **i.** play the piano.

___ **10.** Secretaries   **j.** teach.

B. CROSSWORD

ACROSS

1. We're painters. We _____ houses.

2. I'm a salesperson. I _____ cars.

3. He's a singer. He likes to _____ .

4. I'm a secretary. I can _____ very fast.

5. I'm a reporter. I _____ for a newspaper.

7. We _____ equipment in a factory.

10. I'm a waitress. I _____ food.

DOWN

1. You _____ the piano very well.

3. I _____ clothes with a sewing machine.

6. I can _____ things when they're broken.

8. I'm a teacher. I _____ Spanish.

9. They _____ dishes in a restaurant.

A. MATCHING

_c_ **1.** time   **a.** office
___ **2.** conveyor   **b.** belt
___ **3.** freight   **c.** cards
___ **4.** suggestion   **d.** line
___ **5.** personnel   **e.** elevator
___ **6.** assembly   **f.** box

___ **7.** vending   **g.** room
___ **8.** fire   **h.** clock
___ **9.** supply   **i.** extinguisher
___**10.** safety   **j.** office
___**11.** time   **k.** machine
___**12.** payroll   **l.** glasses

B. WHICH WORD?

1. Are you wearing your (conveyor belt (mask))?
2. Can you drive a (hand truck   forklift)?
3. You can get your checks in the (payroll office   supply room).
4. Put the boxes in the (suggestion box   freight elevator).
5. Sylvia had an accident. We need the (first-aid kit   safety glasses).
6. Pull the (forklift   lever) to stop the machine.
7. Jeff works in the (loading dock   warehouse).

C. AT THE FACTORY

box   cafeteria   card   clock   foreman   glasses   line   machine   mask   room   station

Sally works in a large factory. Every day she takes a time _____card_____ 1

and punches the time _____ 2. She gets her safety _____ 3

and _____ 4 from the supply _____ 5 and goes to her work

_____ 6 on the assembly _____ 7. She always says hello

to the _____ 8.

At noon Sally usually has lunch in the _____ 9. But she isn't

eating there today. Today she's getting a sandwich and soda from the vending

_____ 10. During lunch she's going to write a note about a problem

in the factory and put it in the suggestion _____ 11.

THE CONSTRUCTION SITE

A. WHICH GROUP?

backhoe	bulldozer	cement mixer	front-end loader	plywood
brick	cement	dump truck	lumber	

Building materials:

- _____brick_____
- _____
- _____
- _____

Vehicles:

- _____backhoe_____
- _____
- _____
- _____
- _____

B. YES OR NO?

Look at page 152 of the Basic Picture Dictionary. Answer *Yes* or *No*.

Yes **1.** There's a ladder next to the building.

_____ **2.** A man is standing on the ladder.

_____ **3.** There's a wheelbarrow in front of the ladder.

_____ **4.** There are bricks in the wheelbarrow.

_____ **5.** A worker is sitting on the scaffolding.

_____ **6.** The front-end loader is next to the dump truck.

_____ **7.** There's lumber in the dump truck.

_____ **8.** There's a backhoe next to the front-end loader.

_____ **9.** The bulldozer is mixing cement.

_____ **10.** A worker is carrying lumber.

_____ **11.** A man is standing near the backhoe.

_____ **12.** The workers are wearing helmets.

C. WHICH WORD?

1. You have to wear a (backhoe (helmet)) at the construction site.

2. John drives a (bulldozer   wheelbarrow).

3. There's water on the floor because the (pipes   wires) are broken.

4. The shingles on our house are made of (brick   wood).

5. Our house is very warm because we have a lot of (insulation   beams) in the walls.

6. Go up on the (front-end loader   scaffolding) when you paint the house.

A. WHERE DO THEY GO?

battery	engine	flare	jumper cables	spare tire
carburetor	fan belt	jack	radiator	spark plugs

Under the hood:

In the trunk:

- <u>   battery   </u>
- _____
- _____

- _____
- _____
- _____

- _____
- _____
- _____
- _____

B. MATCHING: *WHAT'S THE WORD?*

<u>b</u> **1.** jumper   **a.** plate

___ **2.** windshield   **b.** cables

___ **3.** license   **c.** wipers

___ **4.** spark   **d.** belt

___ **5.** fan   **e.** pump

___ **6.** air   **f.** plugs

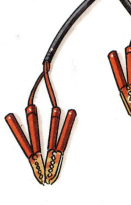

C. MATCHING: *WHAT CAN THEY USE?*

<u>c</u> **1.** "This tire needs air."

___ **2.** "This radio doesn't work very well."

___ **3.** "It's starting to rain."

___ **4.** "It's dark. We can't see."

___ **5.** "I need to change a tire."

___ **6.** "Where can I put these suitcases?"

___ **7.** "I can't see out the back window."

a. windshield wipers

b. trunk

c. air pump

d. jack

e. headlights

f. rear defroster

g. antenna

D. LISTENING: *REPAIR CHECKLIST*

Listen to the repairperson. Check the items that were replaced or fixed.

___ spark plugs	___ rear defroster
✓ fan belt	___ taillights
___ carburetor	___ windshield wipers
___ battery	___ headlights
___ tires	___ radiator

A. MATCHING: *WHAT'S THE WORD?*

_c_ 1. manual
___ 2. seat
___ 3. shoulder
___ 4. rearview
___ 5. steering

a. belt
b. column
c. transmission
d. mirror
e. harness

___ 6. emergency
___ 7. turn
___ 8. gas
___ 9. glove
___ 10. air

f. signal
g. compartment
h. bag
i. pedal
j. brake

B. WHAT'S BROKEN?

brakes   radio   speedometer   turn signal
glove compartment   rearview mirror   steering column   visor

1. Let's listen to some music.   We can't. The ___radio___ is broken!

2. How fast are we going?   I don't know. The _____ is broken!

3. Do you see the car behind you?   No, I don't. The _____ is broken!

4. You should signal before you turn.   I can't. The _____ is broken!

5. Turn left at the next corner.   I can't. The _____ is broken!

6. Stop the car!   I can't. The _____ are broken!

7. Where can I put these maps?   Sorry. I can't open the _____!

8. I can't see! The sun is in my eyes!   Sorry. The _____ is broken!

A. WHICH WORD?

1. This taxi ride is very expensive! Look at the ((meter) fare card).
2. I need some tokens for the (subway   bus stop).
3. A (baggage   passenger) is waiting for a bus.
4. Put your token in the (token booth   turnstile).
5. The (train   bus) is arriving on Track 5.
6. The (engineer   conductor) checks your tickets.
7. The porter will carry your (luggage   timetable).

B. WHICH WORD DOESN'T BELONG?

1. passenger car   dining car   (porter)   sleeper
2. bus stop   taxi stand   subway station   timetable
3. ticket counter   porter   engineer   conductor
4. cab driver   meter   bus driver   engineer
5. cab   ticket window   meter   taxi stand

C. WHICH WORDS ARE CORRECT?

Circle the correct words.

1. ticket (counter) station (window)
2. passenger dining engine car
3. bus stand station stop
4. taxi stand driver booth
5. Read the schedule turnstile timetable .
6. Talk to the counter conductor porter .

D. LISTENING: *WHERE ARE THEY?*

Listen and circle the correct place.

1. bus station   (train station)
2. subway station   bus station
3. taxi   train
4. subway   taxi
5. train   bus
6. subway station   train station

THE AIRPORT

A. AT THE AIRPORT

| agent | check | counter | monitor | pass | ticket | suitcases |

Tom is carrying two ___suitcases___ 1 and a

_____ 2. He's looking at the arrival and

departure _____ 3. He's going to give his

ticket to the ticket _____ 4 at the ticket

_____ 5. She's going to give him a boarding

_____ 6 and a baggage claim _____ 7

for his suitcases.

| boarding | check-in | checkpoint | detector | guard | waiting | X-ray |

Mrs. Gomez is going to the gate, but first
she needs to stop at the security _____ 8.
The security _____ 9 is going to use the
_____ 10 machine to look in her bag.
Then Mrs. Gomez is going to walk through the
metal _____ 11. She's going to show her
ticket and her _____ 12 pass to the agent
at the _____ 13 counter at the gate. Then
she's going to sit in the _____ 14 area.

| baggage claim | customs declaration | customs officer | garment | suitcase |

Rhoda is in the _____ 15 area.

She's carrying a _____ 16 and a

_____ 17 bag. The _____ 18

is going to look in Rhoda's suitcase and take her

_____ 19 form.

B. WHICH WORDS ARE CORRECT?

Circle the correct words.

1. ticket **counter** / ~~agent~~ / officer

2. **waiting** / suitcase / baggage claim area

3. customs / immigration / boarding officer

4. passport / check-in / ticket counter

5. security detector / guard / checkpoin

6. baggage claim area / monitor / check

C. OUT OF ORDER!

You're at the airport. Put the actions in order.

___ Give your ticket to the ticket agent.
___ Put your bag on the X-ray machine.
___ Wait for your airplane at the gate.
_1_ Go to the ticket counter.
___ Go to the security checkpoint.
___ Walk through the metal detector.

___ Go to the baggage claim area.
___ Go to customs.
_1_ Get off the plane.
___ Leave the airport.
___ See the customs officer.
___ Get your suitcases.

1.   2.

D. WHICH WORD?

1. You can get a boarding pass at the (**check-in counter**   arrival and departure monitor).
2. Wait for your plane at the (baggage claim area   gate).
3. Don't forget to sign the (customs declaration form   baggage claim check).
4. Give your (passport   boarding pass) to the immigration officer.
5. Show your (garment bag   metal detector) to the security guard.

E. LISTENING: *WHERE ARE THEY?*

Listen and choose the correct place.

1. customs   **ticket counter**
2. immigration   waiting area
3. baggage claim area   security checkpoint
4. baggage claim area   ticket counter
5. security checkpoint   check-in counter
6. customs   immigration

A. WHICH WORD?

1. Put on your coat. It's ((cold) warm) outside.

2. I think it's going to rain this afternoon. It's very (cloudy cool).

3. We can't see very well because it's (muggy foggy).

4. There's going to be a hurricane tomorrow. It's going to be very (windy tornado).

5. I like cold weather. (Summer Winter) is my favorite season.

6. Look at the lightning. There's going to be a (snowstorm thunderstorm).

7. The rain is beginning to freeze. It's (sleeting drizzling).

8. The weather is clear and (hazy cold).

9. It's a cloudy, humid, (sunny muggy) day.

10. The temperature is 32 degrees (Fahrenheit thermometer). It's (hot freezing).

B. WHICH WORD DOESN'T BELONG?

1.	hot	cool	(windy)	warm
2.	hurricane	thermometer	thunderstorm	tornado
3.	lightning	sleeting	snowing	hailing
4.	cloudy	clear	hazy	foggy
5.	summer	spring	Fahrenheit	autumn

C. LISTENING: *THE WORLD-WIDE WEATHER FORECAST*

Listen to the World-Wide Weather forecast and check *Yes* or *No*.

		Yes	No
1.	It's going to be cloudy and warm in France.	____	✓
2.	It's going to be hot and foggy in Spain.	____	____
3.	It's going to be cold and windy in Russia.	____	____
4.	It's going to be warm in Sweden.	____	____
5.	There are going to be thunderstorms in Japan.	____	____
6.	It's going to be foggy and cool in Korea.	____	____
7.	It's going to be very windy in the United States.	____	____

A. WHICH WORD?

1. My favorite winter sport is (skiing   roller skating).
2. I really like to play (skating   football).
3. I like to go (skiing   fishing) in the lake near my house.
4. Do you want to go (bicycling   tennis) with me this weekend?
5. I feel tired today. I won't go jogging. I think I'll go (running   walking).
6. I enjoy water sports. I really like (swimming   skiing) and (jogging   sailing).

B. CROSSWORD

ACROSS

1.

3.

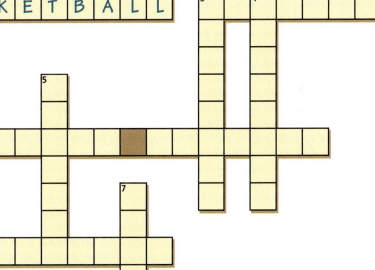

6.    8.    9.

DOWN

1.    2.    3.    4.    5.    7.

WORKBOOK PAGES 1–2

A. WHAT'S THE WORD?

1. first
2. middle
3. last
4. area
5. telephone
6. address
7. city
8. state
9. apartment
10. zip

B. WHAT'S THE ANSWER?

1. b
2. a
3. d
4. e
5. c
6. g
7. f

C. LISTENING: *WHAT'S THE ANSWER?*

Circle the correct answer.

1. What's your first name?
2. What's your apartment number?
3. What state?
4. What's your address?
5. What's your zip code?
6. What's the area code?

Answers

1. John
2. 3B
3. Texas
4. 13 Maple Drive
5. 11375
6. 212

WORKBOOK PAGES 3–4

A. WHO ARE THEY?

1. husband
2. mother
3. son
4. sister
5. grandfather
6. granddaughter

B. MATCHING: *WHO ARE THEY?*

1. c
2. a
3. d
4. b

C. WHICH WORD?

1. father
2. sister
3. son
4. wife
5. grandson
6. brother
7. grandchildren

D. HIS OR HER?

1. His
2. Her
3. Her
4. His
5. Her
6. His

E. MEET OUR FAMILY

1. wife
2. daughter
3. son
4. brother
5. grandson
6. granddaughter

WORKBOOK PAGE 5

A. WHO ARE THEY?

1. uncle
2. niece
3. father-in-law
4. son-in-law
5. sister-in-law

B. MEET OUR FAMILY

1. son
2. brother
3. niece
4. uncle
5. nephew
6. daughter-in-law
7. son-in-law
8. sister-in-law

WORKBOOK PAGE 6

A. WHICH ROOM?

Bathroom:
brush my teeth
floss my teeth
shave
take a shower
wash my face

Bedroom:
get up
go to bed
make the bed
sleep

Kitchen:
cook dinner
eat breakfast
eat dinner
have lunch
make breakfast

C. WHICH WORD?

1. hair
2. makeup
3. bed
4. dinner
5. lunch
6. dressed
7. wash
8. have
9. brush
10. get
11. take
12. make

WORKBOOK PAGE 7

A. WHICH WORD?

1. feeding
2. listening to
3. sweeping
4. practicing
5. doing
6. washing

B. WHAT'S THE ACTION?

1. feeding
2. reading
3. ironing
4. playing

C. CROSSWORD (see p. 117)

WORKBOOK PAGES 8–9

A. WHICH WORD?

1. globe, pencil
2. computer
3. textbook, desk
4. paper, chalk
5. board
6. eraser, tray
7. map
8. flag
9. desk
10. clock

B. MATCHING: *WHAT'S THE WORD?*

1. notebook
2. thumbtack
3. loudspeaker
4. bookshelf

C. CROSSWORD (see p. 117)

WORKBOOK PAGE 10

A. WHICH WORD?

1. up
2. Write
3. name
4. board
5. Read
6. book
7. teacher
8. groups
9. page
10. book

B. OUT OF ORDER!

1.	2.
2	5
1	2
4	4
3	1
5	3

C. YOU'RE THE TEACHER!

Possible sentences:

Close your book.
Erase your answer.
Erase your name.
Erase your question.
Open your book.
Put away your book.
Read your answer.
Read your book.
Read your name.
Read your question.
Write your answer.
Write your name.
Write your question.

WORKBOOK PAGE 11

A. WHAT'S THE ACTION?

1. Collect
2. Take
3. Bring in
4. Hand in
5. Correct
6. Take out
7. Lower
8. Go over

B. LISTENING: *WHAT'S THE WORD?*

Listen and circle the words you hear.

1. Pass out the tests.
2. Lower the shades.
3. Check your homework.
4. Collect the tests.
5. Turn on the projector.
6. Go over your homework.

Answers

1. Pass out
2. Lower
3. Check
4. Collect
5. Turn on
6. Go over

WORKBOOK PAGE 12

A. WHERE DO THEY LIVE?

1. condominium
2. mobile home
3. dormitory
4. apartment building
5. farmhouse
6. houseboat
7. cabin
8. nursing home

B. MATCHING

1. d
2. f
3. g
4. c
5. a
6. e
7. b

WORKBOOK PAGE 13

A. WHERE ARE THEY?

1. lamp
2. end table
3. pillow
4. coffee table
5. painting
6. photograph
7. mantel
8. curtains
9. stereo, speaker*, VCR*, television*

*These can be in any order.

B. LISTENING: *YES OR NO?*

Look at page 20 of the Basic Picture Dictionary. Listen to the questions and circle *Yes* or *No*.

1. Is there a rug on the floor?
2. Is there a book on the mantel?
3. Is there a VCR in the wall unit?
4. Is there a plant on the coffee table?
5. Is there a photograph on the bookcase?
6. Is there a lamp in the entertainment unit?
7. Are there drapes on the window?
8. Is there a pillow on the loveseat?
9. Is there a picture on the end table?

Answers

1. Yes
2. No
3. Yes
4. No
5. Yes
6. No
7. Yes
8. No
9. No

C. WHICH WORD DOESN'T BELONG?

1. end table (The others are things you sit on.)
2. bookcase (The others are related to a fireplace.)
3. lampshade (The others are related to windows.)
4. plant (The others are home entertainment items.)
5. pillow (The others are things in frames.)
6. speaker (The others are parts of a room.)

WORKBOOK PAGE 14

A. WHERE ARE THEY?

On the buffet:
pitcher
salad bowl
serving bowl
serving platter

On the serving cart:
coffee pot
creamer
sugar bowl
teapot

On the table:
butter dish
candlestick
centerpiece
pepper shaker
salt shaker
tablecloth

B. MATCHING: *WHERE ARE THEY?*

1. e
2. a
3. d
4. c
5. b

C. MATCHING: *WHAT'S THE WORD?*

1. candlestick
2. tablecloth
3. teapot
4. centerpiece

D. LISTENING: *FINISH THE SENTENCE*

Listen and choose the correct word.

1. I'd like some butter. Please pass the butter. . .
2. I'd like some salad. Please pass the salad . . .
3. I'd like some water. Please pass the . . .
4. I'd like some pepper. Please pass the . . .
5. I'd like some coffee. Please pass the . . .
6. I'd like some cream in my coffee. Please pass the . . .

Answers

1. dish
2. bowl
3. pitcher
4. shaker
5. coffee pot
6. creamer

WORKBOOK PAGE 15

A. FINISH THE PLACE SETTING

1. teaspoon
2. soup bowl
3. dinner fork
4. cup
5. salad plate
6. butter knife

B. WHICH WORDS ARE CORRECT?

1. dinner, salad
2. salad, dinner
3. bowl, spoon

WORKBOOK PAGE 16

A. MATCHING: *WHERE ARE THEY?*

1. d
2. c
3. a
4. f
5. b
6. e

B. WHICH WORD DOESN'T BELONG?

1. footboard (The others are pieces of furniture.)
2. nightstand (The others are types of beds.)
3. comforter (The others are types of beds.)
4. pillowcase (The others are types of blankets.)
5. jewelry box (The others are parts of a bed.)
6. blinds (The others go on the bed.)

C. LISTENING: *WHICH ROOM?*

Listen and circle the letter of the room these people are talking about.

1. Please close the blinds.
2. Please turn off the electric blanket.
3. The bedroom has a double bed.
4. It's in the jewelry box on the nightstand.
5. Please turn off the alarm.
6. Susie can sleep on the cot.
7. I don't have a pillowcase.
8. Your shirt is in the dresser.

Answers

1. B
2. A
3. A
4. B
5. A
6. A
7. B
8. A

WORKBOOK PAGE 17

A. WHICH GROUP?

These are for cleaning:
dishwasher detergent
dish towel
garbage disposal
pot scrubber
scouring pad
sink
sponge

These are for cooking:
cookbook
microwave
oven
potholder
range
stove
toaster

B. WHICH WORD?

1. spice
2. disposal
3. pot scrubber
4. dishwasher
5. can opener
6. placemats
7. counter
8. tray, freezer

C. WHICH WORD DOESN'T BELONG?

1. faucet (The others are parts of a refrigerator.)
2. canister (The others are for garbage or trash.)
3. sink (The others are cleaning items.)
4. potholder (The others are appliances.)
5. dish rack (The others are appliances.)

WORKBOOK PAGE 18

A. WHICH GROUP?

Places where the baby sits:	Things the baby plays with:
baby carrier	doll
baby seat	mobile
booster seat	rattle
car seat	stuffed animal
high chair	teddy bear
playpen	
stroller	
swing	
walker	

B. MATCHING: *WHERE ARE THEY?*

1. e
2. d
3. b
4. f
5. c
6. g
7. a

C. LISTENING

Listen and choose the correct picture.

1. A. Where's Tommy?
   B. He's in the cradle.
2. A. Where's Lisa?
   B. She's sitting in her high chair.
3. A. Where's the stuffed animal?
   B. It's in the toy chest.
4. A. Where's Susie?
   B. She's in the baby carriage.
5. A. Where's Billy?
   B. He's in the walker.
6. A. Thank you for the doll. It's a very nice gift.
   B. I'm glad you like it.

Answers

1. _____ ✓   2. _____ ✓   3. ✓ _____
4. _____ ✓   5. ✓ _____   6. ✓ _____

WORKBOOK PAGE 19

A. WHERE DO THEY GO?

These go in the baby's mouth:	These go on the baby's body:
formula	baby lotion
nipple	baby powder
pacifier	ointment
teething ring	
vitamins	

B. WHAT'S THE WORD?

1. formula, nipple
2. teething ring
3. baby shampoo
4. cotton swabs
5. baby food
6. bib
7. pins, disposable
8. baby powder

C. LISTENING: WHICH BABY?

Listen and decide which baby they're talking about.

1. Where are the diaper pins?
2. Please pass the baby lotion.
3. Please open the baby food.
4. Billy likes his pacifier.
5. That's a very nice bib.
6. Are there any vitamins in the formula?
7. We need some more ointment.
8. Do we need a new nipple?

Answers

1. A   5. B
2. A   6. B
3. B   7. A
4. A   8. B

WORKBOOK PAGE 20

A. MATCHING: WHERE ARE THEY?

1. e   5. a
2. c   6. d
3. g   7. b
4. f

B. WHICH WORD?

1. toilet brush   5. Water Pik
2. sponge   6. mirror
3. hair dryer   7. rubber mat
4. medicine chest

C. WHICH WORDS ARE CORRECT?

1. cabinet, chest
2. rubber, bath
3. seat, paper

D. LISTENING: FINISH THE SENTENCE

Listen and choose the correct answer.

1. Put the towel in the . . .
2. Look in the medicine . . .
3. I'd really like to take a bath in my new . . .
4. I'm looking for the air . . .
5. My hair is wet. Where's the . . . ?
6. The towels are over there on the . . .

Answers

1. hamper   4. freshener
2. cabinet   5. hair dryer
3. bathtub   6. towel rack

WORKBOOK PAGES 21–22

A. WHERE DO THEY GO?

Hair care products:	Dental care products:
brush	dental floss
comb	mouthwash
conditioner	toothbrush
hairspray	toothpaste
shampoo	

Shaving products:

after shave lotion
electric razor
razor
razor blades
shaving creme

B. MATCHING: WHAT'S THE WORD?

1. e   5. b
2. g   6. d
3. a   7. c
4. f

C. LISTENING

Listen and circle the word you hear.

1. Excuse me. Where can I find nail polish?
2. Excuse me. Where can I find dental floss?
3. Where's my toothbrush?
4. Excuse me. Where can I find hairspray?
5. Excuse me. Where can I find shoe polish?
6. Where's my electric shaver?

Answers

1. nail polish	4. hairspray
2. dental floss	5. shoe polish
3. toothbrush	6. electric shaver

D. WHICH WORD IS CORRECT?

1. polish
2. shower
3. clipper
4. floss

E. CROSSWORD (see p. 118)

WORKBOOK PAGE 23

A. MATCHING: WHERE ARE THEY?

1. f	4. a
2. e	5. d
3. c	6. b

B. WHICH WORD?

1. basket	4. vacuum
2. iron	5. clothesline
3. mop	6. recycling bin

C. WHICH WORDS ARE CORRECT?

1. broom vacuum	3. dryer trash can
2. iron vacuum	4. sponge scrub brush

D. LISTENING: YES OR NO?

Look at page 38 of the Basic Picture Dictionary. Listen to the question and circle Yes or No.

1. Is there a scrub brush on the sink?
2. Are there clothes in the laundry basket?
3. Are there clothespins on the clothesline?
4. Is the dustpan in front of the utility sink?
5. Is the recycling bin next to the bucket?
6. Are there paper towels over the sink?
7. Is there a sponge on the washer?
8. Is the iron next to the trash can?

Answers

1. No	5. Yes
2. Yes	6. Yes
3. Yes	7. No
4. No	8. No

WORKBOOK PAGE 24

A. WHAT'S THE WORD?

1. lamppost	5. driveway
2. doorbell	6. deck
3. TV antenna	7. patio
4. shutters	8. tool shed

B. MATCHING: THEY GO TOGETHER

1. e	5. b
2. g	6. d
3. a	7. f
4. c	

C. WHICH WORD?

1. mailbox	5. porch
2. garage	6. barbecue
3. deck	7. shutters
4. doorbell	8. satellite dish

WORKBOOK PAGE 25

A. WHICH WORD?

1. chute	5. superintendent
2. lock	6. lobby
3. storage room	7. air conditioner
4. smoke detector	

B. MY APARTMENT BUILDING

1. buzzer	7. air conditioner
2. lobby	8. pool
3. intercom	9. laundry room
4. elevator	10. parking garage
5. peephole	11. superintendent
6. balcony	

C. LISTENING

Listen and circle the word you hear.

1. The superintendent is fixing the intercom.
2. I'm waiting for you in the lobby.
3. Is your car in the parking lot?
4. No, it's in the garage.
5. There are a lot of people in the pool today.
6. Please put these in the storage room.

Answers

1. intercom	4. garage
2. lobby	5. pool
3. lot	6. storage

WORKBOOK PAGE 26

A. WHO ARE THEY?

1. chimney sweep	6. electrician*
2. handyman	7. plumber*
3. painter	8. exterminator*
4. appliance repair person	9. locksmith
	10. gardener
5. TV repair person	11. carpenter

*Note: These three answers can be for 6, 7, or 8.

B. WHO SHOULD THEY CALL?

1. TV repair person
2. locksmith
3. chimney sweep
4. plumber
5. exterminator
6. painter
7. carpenter
8. handyman

WORKBOOK PAGES 27–28

A. WHAT'S THE TOOL?

1. b		4. a	
2. c		5. c	
3. b		6. a	

B. WHICH WORD?

1. hose		5. saw
2. shovel		6. wrench
3. flashlight		7. nail
4. wheelbarrow		

C. MATCHING: *WHAT'S THE WORD?*

1. screwdriver		4. sandpaper
2. flashlight		5. wheelbarrow
3. paintbrush		6. lawnmower

D. WHICH WORD DOESN'T BELONG?

1. paint roller (The others are used for gardening.)
2. step ladder (The others are tools.)
3. vise (The others are for fastening things.)
4. hose (The others are tools.)
5. sandpaper (The others are for fastening things.)

E. CROSSWORD (see p. 118)

WORKBOOK PAGE 29

A. MATCHING

1. c		5. g
2. a		6. h
3. d		7. f
4. b		8. e

B. WHAT'S THE NUMBER?

1. 6		7. 25
2. 12		8. 33
3. 18		9. 72
4. 15		10. 67
5. 40		11. 200
6. 90		12. 1000

C. WHAT'S THE WORD?

one	twenty
five	thirty
eight	fifty-six
eleven	ninety-four
seventeen	one hundred

D. LISTENING: *CIRCLE THE NUMBER*

Listen and circle the number you hear.
1. I'm thirty years old.
2. My address is Forty Main Street.
3. I'm fifteen years old.
4. I'm sixty years old.
5. My address is Seventeen School Street.
6. There are eighteen students in my class.
7. My address is Ninety River Street.
8. I have thirty-five dollars.
9. I have sixty-six dollars.
10. My address is Twenty-One Center Street.

Answers

1. 30	5. 17	8. 35
2. 40	6. 18	9. 66
3. 15	7. 90	10. 21
4. 60		

WORKBOOK PAGE 30

A. MATCHING

1. b		5. g
2. d		6. h
3. a		7. f
4. c		8. e

B. WHAT'S THE NUMBER?

1. 1st		6. 33rd
2. 11th		7. 16th
3. 7th		8. 60th
4. 2nd		9. 59th
5. 44th		10. 95th

C. LISTENING: *WHERE DO THEY LIVE?*

Listen and circle the number you hear.
1. I live on the eighteenth floor.
2. I live on Fortieth Street.
3. I live on the thirty-first floor.
4. I live on Nineteenth Street.
5. I live on the twenty-second floor.
6. I live on One Hundred and Fifth Street.
7. I live on West Eighth Street.
8. I live on Sixtieth Street.

Answers

1. 18th		5. 22nd
2. 40th		6. 105th
3. 31st		7. 8th
4. 19th		8. 60th

D. THEY GO TOGETHER

1. first		4. fifteenth
2. third		5. fifth
3. tenth		6. twenty-second

E. LISTENING: *WHAT'S MY NAME?*

Listen and fill in the letters where they belong.

The first letter of my name is F.
The third letter is A.
The fifth letter is K.
The seventh letter is I.
The sixth letter is L.
The second letter is R.
The fourth letter is N.
The eighth letter is N.

Answer

F R A N K L I N

WORKBOOK PAGES 31–32

A. WHAT'S THE WORD?

1. subtraction
2. addition
3. multiplication
4. division

B. MATCHING: *WHAT'S THE SIGN?*

1. b
2. a
3. d
4. e
5. c

C. MATH SENTENCES

1. 6 plus 2 equals 8.
2. 6 minus 2 equals 4.
3. 6 times 2 equals 12.
4. 6 divided by 2 equals 3.

D. WHAT'S THE PROBLEM?

$$\begin{array}{r} 5 \\ -2 \\ \hline 3 \end{array} \qquad \begin{array}{r} 7 \\ +2 \\ \hline 9 \end{array} \qquad \begin{array}{r} 6 \\ \times 2 \\ \hline 12 \end{array} \qquad 12 \div 3 = 4$$

1.   2.   3.   4.

E. LISTENING

Listen and write the number under the correct math problem.

1. How much is three times three?
2. How much is three minus three?
3. How much is three divided by three?
4. How much is three plus three?

Answers

2 4 1 3

F. MATCHING

1. d
2. b
3. a
4. e
5. c
6. h
7. f
8. i
9. g

G. LISTENING: *WHAT'S THE FRACTION?*

Listen and write the number under the correct fraction.

1. A. Is this on sale?
   B. Yes. It's one third off the regular price.
2. A. How much is this?
   B. It's one fourth off the regular price.
3. A. How much is this?
   B. It's two thirds off the regular price.
4. A. Is the gas tank almost empty?
   B. No. It's three quarters full.
5. A. Are all the students here today?
   B. No. One half of the students are absent.

Answers

2 1 5 3 4

H. LISTENING: *WHAT'S THE PERCENT?*

Listen and write the number under the correct percent.

1. A. What's the weather forecast?
   B. There's a seventy-five percent chance of rain tomorrow.
2. A. What's the weather forecast?
   B. There's a twenty-five percent chance of rain.
3. A. I got one hundred percent on the test yesterday.
   B. That's great.
4. A. How much is this?
   B. It's fifty percent off the regular price.

Answers

2 4 1 3

WORKBOOK PAGE 33

A. WHAT TIME IS IT?

1.   2.   3.   4.

5.   6.   7.   8.

B. WHICH TIMES ARE CORRECT?

1. b, c
2. a, c
3. a, c
4. b, c
5. a, b
6. a, c

C. LISTENING: *WHICH CLOCK?*

Listen and write the number under the correct clock.

1. A. When do you eat dinner?
   B. I eat dinner at 6:30.
2. A. What time does the train arrive?
   B. It arrives at 5:15.
3. A. What time does the movie begin?
   B. It begins at 6:40.
4. A. What time is it?
   B. It's 5:05.
5. A. What time do you get up?
   B. I get up at half past five.
6. A. What time does the bus arrive?
   B. It arrives at a quarter to seven.

Answers

4 2 5 1 3 6

WORKBOOK PAGE 34

A. OUT OF ORDER: *MONTHS*
10
1
9
7
11
6
2
4
3
12
8
5

B. OUT OF ORDER: *DAYS*
4
7
2
6
1
5
3

C. MATCHING
1. c
2. a
3. b
4. d

D. LISTENING
Listen and circle the word you hear.
1. Today is Sunday.
2. I have English class on Thursday.
3. My birthday is June fourth.
4. My sister's birthday is September twenty-seventh.
5. My birthday is in May.
6. Tomorrow is January tenth.

Answers
1. Sunday
2. Thursday
3. June
4. September
5. May
6. January

WORKBOOK PAGE 35

A. MATCHING: *ASSOCIATIONS*
1. c
2. d
3. b
4. a
5. h
6. f
7. g
8. e

B. A BUSY DAY
1. bank
2. child-care center
3. cleaners
4. barber shop
5. clinic
6. bus station
7. cafeteria
8. book store
9. bakery
10. convenience store

C. LISTENING: *WHERE ARE THEY?*
Listen and circle the correct place.
1. What time does the bus leave?
2. The doctor will see you soon.

3. Do you want some sugar in your coffee?
4. How much is a loaf of bread?
5. It's okay, Tommy. Your mother is going to be here very soon.
6. Let's see. Two bottles of soda and a quart of milk That'll be $3.99.

Answers
1. bus station
2. clinic
3. coffee shop
4. bakery
5. day-care center
6. convenience store

WORKBOOK PAGE 36

A. WHICH WORD?
1. health club
2. florist
3. hair salon
4. hotel
5. drug store
6. grocery store
7. service station
8. hospital
9. department
10. hardware store

B. LISTENING: *WHERE DID MARIA GO?*
Listen and write the number under the correct place.
Maria had a very busy day today.
1. At seven o'clock this morning, Maria got up and went to her health club.
2. After that, she stopped at the drug store to buy a few things.
3. Then she went to the hair salon for a haircut.
4. After that, she stopped at the florist to buy some flowers.
5. Then she went to the hospital to visit her mother.
6. Later, she went to the hardware store to buy some tools that she needed.
7. After that, she stopped at the service station for some gas.
8. And finally, she stopped at the grocery store to buy some food for dinner
Yes. Maria certainly had a busy day today.

Answers
4 7 2
  3 6
1 8 5

WORKBOOK PAGE 37

A. MATCHING: *COMPLETE THE SENTENCE*
1. b
2. g
3. f
4. e
5. a
6. c
7. d

B. A WEEKEND VACATION
1. motel
2. museum
3. pizza shop
4. ice cream shop
5. park
6. music store
7. library
8. pet shop
9. movie theater

C. LISTENING: *WHERE ARE THEY?*

Listen and circle the correct place.

1. A. May I help you?
   B. Yes. I'd like a chocolate ice cream cone.
2. A. May I help you?
   B. Yes. How much is that dog in the window?
3. A. This movie is terrible.
   B. You're right. It is.
4. A. What will you have on your pizza?
   B. I'd like a lot of cheese.
5. A. I really like this painting.
   B. I do, too. The flowers are beautiful.
6. A. Do you have change for the washing machine?
   B. Yes. Here you are.

Answers

1. ice cream shop
2. pet shop
3. movie theater
4. pizza shop
5. museum
6. laundromat

WORKBOOK PAGE 38

A. WHICH WORD?

1. toy store
2. post office
3. theater
4. school
5. supermarket
6. restaurant
7. zoo
8. shopping mall
9. video store

B. CROSSWORD (see p. 119)

(see p. 119)

WORKBOOK PAGE 39

A. WHICH GROUP?

People:
bus driver
cab driver
meter maid
taxi driver

Places:
courthouse
jail
police station

Transportation:
bus
cab
ice cream truck
subway
taxi

B. YES OR NO?

1. No
2. Yes
3. No
4. No
5. No
6. Yes
7. Yes

C. WHICH WORDS ARE CORRECT?

1. trash container
   bench
2. bus
   cab
3. subway
   subway station
4. bus stop
   trash container
5. police station
   bench
6. street light
   parking meter

WORKBOOK PAGE 40

A. WHICH WORD?

1. intersection
2. taxi stand
3. phone booth
4. traffic light
5. fire station
6. newsstand
7. pedestrian

B. YES OR NO?

1. Yes
2. No
3. No
4. Yes
5. Yes
6. Yes
7. No
8. Yes

WORKBOOK PAGE 41

A. MATCHING: *OPPOSITES*

1. d
2. c
3. a
4. b
5. g
6. h
7. f
8. e
9. j
10. l
11. k
12. i
13. o
14. m
15. p
16. n

B. LISTENING: *WHAT'S THE ANSWER?*

Listen and choose the correct answer.

1. Is your brother tall?
2. Is her hair straight?
3. Is his car old?
4. Are his pants tight?
5. Is her car slow?
6. Is that street wide?

Answers

1. a
2. a
3. b
4. b
5. a
6. b

C. WHICH WORD?

1. heavy
2. long
3. new
4. curly
5. narrow
6. dark
7. slow
8. short
9. tight
10. big
11. tall
12. good
13. straight
14. thin

WORKBOOK PAGE 42

A. MATCHING: *OPPOSITES*

1. b
2. d
3. c
4. a
5. h
6. g
7. f
8. e
9. j
10. k
11. i
12. l
13. n
14. m
15. p
16. o

B. WHAT'S THE ANSWER?

1.	empty	5.	open
2.	expensive	6.	hard
3.	shiny	7.	loud
4.	messy	8.	easy

C. LISTENING: *WHICH ONE?*

Listen and write the number under the correct picture.

1. Today's homework is very difficult.
2. My desk is very neat.
3. Your dishes are dirty.
4. These clothes are wet.
5. The door is open.
6. This knife is very dull!

Answers

6 1 4
2 5 3

WORKBOOK PAGE 43

A. LISTENING: *HOW DO THEY FEEL?*

Listen and choose the correct picture.

1. You look unhappy today.
2. I'm really full.
3. I'm feeling sick today.
4. You look annoyed. What's the matter?
5. I'm very hungry today.
6. I'm very upset today.
7. I'm really tired today.
8. You look very disappointed. What happened?

Answers

1. ___ ✓		2. ✓ ___	
3. ✓ ___		4. ___ ✓	
5. ___ ✓		6. ✓ ___	
7. ___ ✓		8. ___ ✓	

WORKBOOK PAGES 44–45

A. CROSSWORD (see p. 119)

C. LISTENING: *HOW DO THEY FEEL?*

Listen. How do these people feel? Circle the best answer.

1. I have an important job interview tomorrow morning.
2. My son Robert is a wonderful student. He works very hard.
3. What time is it? I'm so tired. When is this class going to end?
4. Help! Help! Please help me!
5. Oops! I'm sorry. I made a mistake.
6. Timmy has two dollars. I only have one dollar.
7. Ooh! I can't open this door!
8. Jennifer is going to have a baby?! Really? Are you sure?
9. Billy always comes home at 6:00. Where is he?
10. Class begins at 9:00 . . . I think. No. It begins at 10:00. Well, maybe 9:30. Gee, I don't remember.

Answers

1.	nervous	6.	jealous
2.	proud	7.	frustrated
3.	bored	8.	surprised
4.	scared	9.	worried
5.	embarrassed	10.	confused

WORKBOOK PAGE 46

A. WHICH FRUIT DOESN'T BELONG?

1.	Grapes	4.	Coconuts
2.	Raisins	5.	Figs
3.	Apricots	6.	Limes

B. LISTENING: *WHICH FRUIT?*

Listen and check the fruit these people are talking about.

1. This apricot is delicious!
2. How much is this lemon?
3. These cherries are very sweet!
4. Cantaloupe is my favorite kind of melon.
5. Please pass the grapes.
6. This tangerine is very good.

Answers

1. ___ ✓	2. ___ ✓	3. ✓ ___	
4. ✓ ___	5. ✓ ___	6. ___ ✓	

WORKBOOK PAGE 47

A. CROSSWORD (see p. 120)

WORKBOOK PAGE 48

A. MATCH THE FOODS

1.	e	4.	c
2.	d	5.	f
3.	b	6.	a

B. MATCHING: *WHERE IS IT?*

1.	b	4.	e
2.	d	5.	f
3.	a	6.	c

C. WHICH WORDS ARE CORRECT?

1.	cream cheese	4.	milk
	cottage cheese		orange juice
2.	cream	5.	cheese
	milk		egg
3.	margarine	6.	cream
	butter		cottage

WORKBOOK PAGES 49–50

A. MATCH THE FOODS

1.	e	7.	h
2.	g	8.	b
3.	i	9.	j
4.	c	10.	d
5.	a	11.	f
6.	k		

B. WHERE ARE THEY?

1.	cereal	6.	ketchup
2.	soda	7.	flour
3.	spaghetti	8.	vinegar
4.	coffee	9.	toilet paper
5.	rolls		

C. WHICH WORD DOESN'T BELONG?

1. soy sauce (The others are beverages.)
2. coffee (The others are desserts.)
3. cereal (The others are things you add to foods.)
4. tissues (The others are foods.)
5. soap (The others are paper products.)
6. soup (The others are bread products.)
7. sugar (The others are things you put on a sandwich.)
8. flour (The others are things you pour on a salad.)

D. WHAT CAN THEY USE?

1.	noodles	5.	rolls
2.	mustard	6.	pepper
3.	tea	7.	cookies
4.	juice		

WORKBOOK PAGE 51

A. CROSSWORD (see p. 120)

B. LISTENING: *THE BEST RESPONSE*

Listen and choose the best response.
1. I'm a vegetarian. I don't eat meat.
2. Would you like some clams?
3. Would you like some bacon?
4. My sister is coming for dinner tonight, and she loves seafood!
5. Are we having beef for dinner?
6. Let's make hamburgers for dinner!

Answers

1.	a	4.	b
2.	b	5.	a
3.	a	6.	b

WORKBOOK PAGE 52

A. AT THE SUPERMARKET

1.	shopping cart	6.	bagger
2.	customer	7.	paper bag
3.	checkout counter	8.	checkout line
4.	cash register	9.	cashier
5.	scale	10.	shopping basket

B. OUT OF ORDER!

6
2
3
7
1
4
5

C. WHICH WORDS ARE CORRECT?

1.	bag	4.	paper, plastic
2.	line, counter	5.	cash
3.	shopping	6.	cart, basket

WORKBOOK PAGE 53

A. MATCHING: *THEY GO TOGETHER*

1.	f	5.	d
2.	a	6.	e
3.	g	7.	c
4.	b		

B. CROSSWORD (see p. 121)

C. LISTENING: *FINISH THE SENTENCE*

Listen and circle the correct answer.
1. I'd like a bottle of . . .
2. I'd like a bunch of . . .
3. May I have a bag of . . . ?
4. Please give me a carton of . . .
5. Do you have a dozen . . . ?
6. I need a box of . . .

Answers

1.	salad dressing	4.	orange juice
2.	carrots	5.	eggs
3.	potatoes	6.	cereal

WORKBOOK PAGE 54

A. CROSSWORD (see p. 121)

B. WHICH WORD?

1.	loaf	5.	rolls
2.	pint	6.	pound
3.	package	7.	liters
4.	pound	8.	jar

C. LISTENING: *WHAT ARE THEY TALKING ABOUT?*

Listen and circle the correct answer.
1. How much should I buy — a quart or a half-gallon?
2. May I have two loaves, please?
3. We need another jar.
4. How much do you want — a pint or a quart?
5. I'd like two pounds, please.
6. Do you have another roll?

Answers

1.	milk	4.	ice cream
2.	bread	5.	potatoes
3.	mayonnaise	6.	paper towels

WORKBOOK PAGE 55

A. WHICH WORD?

1.	saute	5.	bake
2.	chop	6.	boil
3.	slice	7.	peel
4.	Mix		

B. WHICH WORD DOESN'T BELONG?

1. beat (The others are ways of cooking food.)
2. grate (The others are ways of cooking food.)
3. pour (The others are ways of cutting.)
4. peel (The others are ways of cooking food.)
5. cook (The others are ways of mixing food.)

C. OUT OF ORDER!

2	2
1	4
4	3
3	1
1.	2.

WORKBOOK PAGE 56

A. FIX THE MENU!

1. donut
2. bagel
3. coffee
4. muffin
5. pastry
6. pizza
7. lemonade
8. hot dog
9. iced tea

B. WHAT SHOULD THEY ORDER?

1. soda
2. biscuit
3. muffin
4. iced tea
5. donut

C. WHICH WORD DOESN'T BELONG?

1. muffin (The others are types of sandwiches.)
2. biscuit (The others are beverages.)
3. milk (The others are things you eat.)
4. coffee (The others are cold beverages.)
5. taco (The others are bread products.)

WORKBOOK PAGE 57

A. MATCHING: *WHAT DO THEY DO?*

1. c
2. d
3. a
4. e
5. b

B. AT THE RESTAURANT

1. table
2. menu
3. high chair
4. booth
5. waiter
6. busboy
7. booster seat
8. waitress
9. cashier
10. dishwasher

C. LISTENING: *YES OR NO?*

Look at page 96 of the Basic Picture Dictionary.
Listen to the questions about the picture and answer
Yes or *No.*

1. Is the busboy in the kitchen?
2. Is the little girl sitting in a high chair?
3. Are two men sitting in a booth?
4. Is the cook talking to the cashier?
5. Is the cashier cleaning the table?
6. Is the waiter carrying food?
7. Is the waitress reading a menu?
8. Is the dishwasher washing dishes?

Answers

1. No
2. Yes
3. Yes
4. No
5. No
6. Yes
7. No
8. Yes

WORKBOOK PAGE 58

A. WHAT'S THE COLOR?

blue   white   red   yellow   green

B. MIX THE COLORS

1. green
2. orange
3. pink
4. gray
5. beige
6. purple

C. LISTENING: *FAVORITE COLORS*

Listen and check these people's favorite colors.

1. My favorite color is blue.
2. My favorite color is yellow.
3. My favorite color is pink.
4. My favorite color is white.
5. My favorite color is dark green.
6. My favorite color is gray.

Answers

1.	✓	___	4.	___	✓
2.	___	✓	5.	___	✓
3.	✓	___	6.	✓	___

WORKBOOK PAGE 59

A. WHICH WORD?

1. shorts
2. sweater
3. shirt
4. jacket
5. shorts
6. a shirt
7. blouse
8. a tie

B. LISTENING: *WHAT ARE THEY TALKING ABOUT?*

Listen and circle the clothing item you hear.

1. A. That's a very nice suit.
   B. Thank you.

2. A. I think I'll wear my sports jacket.
   B. Good idea.

3. A. I really like your new dress.
   B. Thanks a lot.

4. A. Do you like my new skirt?
   B. Yes. It's very nice.

5. A. Put on your new slacks.
   B. Okay.

6. A. Excuse me. Where are the shirts?
   B. Shirts are over there.

Answers

1. suit
2. sports jacket
3. dress
4. skirt
5. slacks
6. shirts

WORKBOOK PAGE 60

A. WHICH GROUP?

Men's underwear:
briefs
boxer shorts
underpants
undershirt

Women's underwear:
bra
panties
slip

Sleepwear:
nightgown
pajamas

Footwear:
boots
sandals
shoes
sneakers

B. WHICH WORD?

1. nightgown
2. boots
3. sneakers
4. shorts
5. a bra
6. sandals
7. a dress
8. pajamas
9. socks

C. WHICH WORD DOESN'T BELONG?

1. pajamas (The others are worn on the legs or feet.)
2. slip (The others are footwear.)
3. stockings (The others are sleepwear.)
4. boots (The others are underwear.)
5. nightgown (The others are underwear.)

WORKBOOK PAGE 61

A. WHICH GROUP?

You wear these when it's cold:
coat
down vest
ear muffs
gloves
jacket
mittens
scarf

You wear these when it rains:
poncho
raincoat
rubbers

You wear these when you exercise:
jogging suit
running shorts
sweatshirt
tee shirt

B. MATCHING: WHERE DO THEY GO?

1. d
2. f
3. e
4. a
5. c
6. b

C. WHICH WORD DOESN'T BELONG?

1. hat (The others are exercise clothing.)
2. swimsuit (The others are for cold weather.)
3. baseball cap (The others are worn on the body.)
4. sunglasses (The others are worn when it rains.)

D. LISTENING: THE BEST RESPONSE

Listen and choose the best answer.

1. I can't find my mittens!
2. I can't find my raincoat!
3. I can't find my jogging suit!
4. I can't find my ear muffs!

Answers
1. a
2. b
3. b
4. a

WORKBOOK PAGE 62

A. MATCHING: THEY GO TOGETHER

1. c
2. e
3. d
4. b
5. a

B. LISTENING: WHAT ARE THEY TALKING ABOUT?

Listen and circle the correct word.

1. A. I think I lost an earring!
   B. That's too bad.
2. A. I can't find my belt!
   B. Here it is!
3. A. Is this your bracelet?
   B. No, it isn't.
4. A. Where are my cuff links?
   B. I don't know.
5. A. Where's my book bag?
   B. Here it is!
6. A. Do you have a dime?
   B. I don't know. I'll look in my wallet.

Answers
1. earring
2. belt
3. bracelet
4. cuff links
5. book bag
6. wallet

C. WHAT'S THE WORD?

1. change purse
2. umbrella
3. briefcase
4. watch
5. pin

D. WHICH WORDS ARE CORRECT?

1. a bracelet
   earrings
2. ring
   wedding band
3. change purse
   wallet
4. book bag
   briefcase
5. a pin
   a necklace
6. key ring
   change purse

WORKBOOK PAGE 63

A. WHAT'S THE WORD?

1. plain
2. low
3. heavy
4. loose
5. long
6. tight

109

B. WHICH WORDS ARE CORRECT?

1. short
   small
2. light
   dark
3. narrow
   wide
4. high
   low
5. plain
   tight
6. heavy
   big

C. LISTENING: *THE BEST ANSWER*

Listen and choose the best answer.

1. Is this skirt too big?
2. Are these pants too large?
3. Are these gloves too small?
4. Do you like these shoes?
5. Are the sleeves too short?
6. Do you like the color?

Answers

1. a
2. a
3. b
4. b
5. a
6. b

WORKBOOK PAGE 64

A. WHAT COIN IS IT?

1. penny
2. quarter
3. dime
4. nickel
5. half dollar
6. silver dollar

B. LISTENING: *HOW MUCH?*

Listen and put a check under the correct coins.

1. A. How much is this?
   B. A half dollar.
   A. A half dollar?
   B. Yes.
2. A. How much is this?
   B. Twenty-five cents.
   A. Twenty-five cents?
   B. Yes.
3. A. How much is this?
   B. Seventy-five cents.
   A. Seventy-five cents?
   B. Yes.
4. A. Excuse me. Do you have fifteen cents?
   B. Yes. Here you are.
5. A. Your change is thirty cents.
   B. Thank you.
6. A. Mom, I need twelve cents.
   B. Here you are.

Answers

1. ✓ ___   2. ___ ✓   3. ✓ ___
4. ___ ✓   5. ___ ✓   6. ✓ ___

C. WHICH IS DIFFERENT?

1. $1.00
2. nickel
3. $25
4. $10
5. 50¢

WORKBOOK PAGE 65

A. MATCHING: *WORDS AND NUMBERS*

1. c
2. a
3. b
4. e
5. f
6. d

B. HOW MUCH IS IT?

1. eleven dollars
2. fifteen dollars
3. thirty dollars
4. ten dollars
5. twenty-six dollars
6. twenty-one dollars

C. HOW MUCH MONEY DO THEY HAVE?

1. $150.00
2. $5.10
3. $25.00
4. $10.25
5. $60.00
6. $40.00
7. $10.00

D. LISTENING: *HOW MUCH?*

Listen and circle the correct amount.

1. A. Excuse me. Do you have twenty-five dollars?
   B. Yes. Here are two tens and a five.
2. A. Can you change a ten-dollar bill?
   B. Yes. Here are two fives.
3. A. How much does that cost?
   B. It costs forty dollars and twenty-five cents.
4. A. Here's your change — six dollars.
   B. Thank you.
5. A. How much does that cost?
   B. It costs three dollars and twenty-five cents.
6. A. How much cash do you have?
   B. I have a twenty-dollar bill and a quarter.

Answers

1. $25.00
2. $10.00
3. $40.25
4. $6.00
5. $3.25
6. $20.25

WORKBOOK PAGE 66

A. WHICH WORD?

1. deposit
2. checkbook
3. withdrawal slip
4. ATM card
5. credit card
6. bank teller
7. bank officer
8. ATM machine

B. WHAT ARE THEY SAYING?

1. bank manager
2. vault
3. check
4. withdrawal slip

WORKBOOK PAGE 67

A. WE HAVE TWO OF THESE!

eye	lip	eyebrow	thigh
elbow	shoulder	leg	cheek
ear	knee		hip

B. FROM TOP TO BOTTOM!

forehead	face	back
eyebrow	neck	waist
eye	shoulder	hip
nose	chest	thigh
mouth	abdomen	knee
chin	leg	calf

C. WHICH WORD?

1. chin
2. mouth
3. waist
4. hips
5. neck, shoulders
6. elbow
7. eyes
8. knee

WORKBOOK PAGE 68

A. YOU'RE THE DOCTOR!

1. spinal cord
2. heart
3. throat
4. stomach
5. wrist
6. toes

B. MATCHING: *WHERE ARE THEY?*

1. d
2. a
3. g
4. b
5. e
6. c
7. f

C. HOW MANY DO WE HAVE?

1. 2	5. 10	9. 2
2. 10	6. 2	10. 1
3. 2	7. 2	11. 2
4. 2	8. 10	12. 2

D. WHICH WORD DOESN'T BELONG?

1. foot (The others are part of the hand.)
2. lungs (The others are part of the foot.)
3. toenail (The others are internal organs.)
4. palm (The others are internal organs.)
5. skin (The others are internal organs.)
6. throat (The others are "extremities".)

WORKBOOK PAGES 69–70

A. WHAT'S THE MATTER WITH THEM?

1. a cold
2. a toothache
3. a backache
4. an earache
5. a fever
6. an insect bite
7. a stiff neck
8. a sunburn
9. the chills

B. WHAT DO THEY HAVE?

1. throat
2. runny
3. bite
4. neck
5. cavity
6. infection

C. LISTENING: *WHAT'S THE MATTER?*

Listen and choose the correct answer.

1. A. What's the matter?
   B. I have a headache.
2. A. What's the matter?
   B. I have a sore throat.
3. A. What's the matter?
   B. I have a cough.
4. A. What's the matter?
   B. I have a virus.
5. A. What's the matter?
   B. I have the chills.
6. A. What's the matter?
   B. I have a runny nose.

Answers

1. headache
2. sore throat
3. cough
4. virus
5. chills
6. runny nose

D. CROSSWORD (see p. 122)

WORKBOOK PAGES 71–72

A. WHAT ARE THEY SAYING?

1. dislocated
2. burned
3. congested
4. bruised
5. sneeze
6. swollen
7. bleeding
8. nauseous, throw up
9. broke
10. dizzy
11. exhausted
12. itchy

B. WHICH WORD DOESN'T BELONG?

1. sneeze (The others are injuries.)
2. bleeding (The others are related to a cold.)
3. burp (The others are injuries.)
4. swollen (The others are ways people "feel".)
5. cut (The others are related to eating or drinking.)

C. LISTENING: *WHAT'S THE MATTER?*

What's the matter? Is it a cold, a stomach virus, or an injury? Listen and circle the correct answer.

1. I sprained my ankle!
2. I'm very congested!
3. I feel nauseous and bloated!
4. I dislocated my shoulder!
5. I'm sneezing a lot!
6. I scratched my eye!
7. I'm going to throw up!
8. I broke my leg!
9. I was coughing all night.
10. I burned my arm!

Answers

1. injury
2. cold
3. stomach virus
4. injury
5. cold
6. injury
7. stomach virus
8. injury
9. cold
10. injury

D. WHAT'S THE WORD?

1. swollen, itchy
2. bloated
3. cut
4. sprain
5. broke
6. scraped
7. nauseous
8. burping

111

E. WHICH WORDS ARE CORRECT?

1. bleeding
   swollen
2. scraped
   scratched
3. bruised
   burned
4. twisted
   sprained
5. hurt
   broke
6. congested
   sneezing

WORKBOOK PAGE 73

A. WHO SHOULD THEY CALL?

1. a dentist
2. an optometrist
3. a pediatrician
4. a cardiologist
5. a surgeon
6. an obstetrician

B. WHAT WILL THEY DO?

1. stethoscope
2. thermometer
3. adhesive tape
4. eye chart
5. Novocaine
6. scale
7. examination table
8. X-ray machine

C. LISTENING: *WHO'S TALKING?*

Listen and circle the correct person.

1. Step over here to the X-ray machine.
2. Please open your mouth. I'm going to clean your teeth.
3. Please hand me the drill.
4. Johnny, I'm going to listen to your heart.
5. Please step on the scale.
6. Can you read the eye chart?
7. Tell me about the problems with your family.
8. Congratulations, Mrs. Ortega! You have a beautiful baby girl!

Answers

1. X-ray technician
2. hygienist
3. dentist
4. pediatrician
5. nurse
6. optometrist
7. psychiatrist
8. obstetrician

WORKBOOK PAGE 74

A. WHICH WORD?

1. fluids
2. bandaid
3. gown
4. cast
5. crutches
6. I.V.
7. call button
8. an injection
9. rest
10. diet
11. prescription
12. bed pan

B. IN THE HOSPITAL

1. bed control
2. call button
3. hospital gown
4. tests
5. injection
6. rest
7. fluids
8. I.V.
9. therapy
10. crutches

WORKBOOK PAGE 75

A. MATCHING: *WHAT DO I NEED?*

1. d
2. f
3. e
4. a
5. c
6. b

B. WHICH WORD DOESN'T BELONG?

1. teaspoon (The others are pills.)
2. decongestant (The others are for the skin.)
3. tablespoon (The others are medicines.)
4. ice pack (The others are pills.)

C. LISTENING: *WHAT'S THE WORD?*

Listen and circle the word you hear.

1. Here. Take these two capsules.
2. Take one teaspoon of cough syrup at night.
3. Here are some lozenges for your throat.
4. Take one caplet every four hours.
5. Take one teaspoon every three hours.
6. Put this heating pad on your shoulder.

Answers

1. capsules
2. syrup
3. lozenges
4. caplet
5. teaspoon
6. pad

D. WHICH WORDS ARE CORRECT?

1. cold
   antacid
2. drops
   syrup
3. eye
   cough
4. tablets
   caplets
5. decongestant
   nasal
6. lotion
   creme

WORKBOOK PAGE 76

A. MATCHING: *FINISH THE WORDS*

1. c
2. a
3. b
4. e
5. f
6. d

B. WHICH WORD?

1. a mail truck
2. aerogramme
3. letter carrier
4. money order
5. postal clerk
6. express
7. address
8. change-of-address

C. WHICH WORDS ARE CORRECT?

1. a roll
   a sheet
2. air mail
   first class
3. envelope
   postcard
4. address
   zip code
5. a package
   an aerogramme
6. clerk
   worker
7. express
   registered
8. stamp
   money order

WORKBOOK PAGE 77

A. WHAT ARE THEY SAYING?

1. shelves
2. library
3. atlas
4. card catalog
5. librarian
6. newspaper
7. dictionary

B. WHICH WORDS ARE CORRECT?

1. card, assistant
2. information, checkout
3. call, library

C. OUT OF ORDER!

3
5
7
2
1
6
4

WORKBOOK PAGE 78

A. WHICH WORD?

1. school nurse
2. guidance counselor
3. track
4. locker
5. custodian
6. field
7. driver's ed instructor
8. principal

B. WHERE ARE THEY?

1. language lab
2. auditorium
3. cafeteria
4. chemistry lab
5. bleachers
6. locker room
7. gym
8. classroom

C. LISTENING: *WHO'S TALKING?*

Listen and decide who is speaking.

1. Do you have a headache? I'm going to take your temperature.
2. Run around the track. You need to exercise before the football game.
3. I understand you're having problems in school. Tell me about them.
4. Your teacher says you don't listen. I'm going to talk to your parents.
5. I have to clean the auditorium now.
6. Stop the car! The light is red!

Answers

1. school nurse
2. coach
3. guidance counselor
4. principal
5. custodian
6. driver's ed instructor

WORKBOOK PAGE 79

A. WHAT SUBJECTS SHOULD THEY STUDY?

1. health
2. Spanish
3. science
4. history
5. art
6. music
7. math
8. geography
9. home economics
10. English

WORKBOOK PAGE 80

A. CROSSWORD (see p. 122)

B. LISTENING: *WHICH ACTIVITY?*

Listen and write the number next to the correct activity.

1. (sound: choir music)
2. "And Kelly kicks the ball! It's a touchdown!"
3. (sound: band music)
4. "Romeo, Romeo. You are the sun and the moon and the stars."
5. "There are many problems in our school this year. We need to talk about them."

Answers

3 1 4 2 5

WORKBOOK PAGE 81

A. WHAT DO THEY USE?

1. d
2. f
3. e
4. a
5. c
6. b

B. WHAT'S THE OCCUPATION?

1. bricklayer
2. butcher
3. bus driver
4. actress
5. cashier
6. carpenter
7. accountant

C. LISTENING: *WHO'S TALKING?*

Listen and circle the correct job.

1. Here's your change. Have a nice day.
2. Do you want a shampoo before I cut your hair?
3. Next stop — Main Street!
4. What kind of meat do you want today — steak or chicken?
5. Well, I fixed your steps. Now I'll fix your front door.
6. Oh, Susan! Please don't go! I love you very much!

Answers

1. cashier
2. barber
3. bus driver
4. butcher
5. carpenter
6. actor

WORKBOOK PAGE 82

A. WHAT'S THE OCCUPATION?

1. fisherman
2. foreman
3. chef
4. housekeeper
5. hairdresser
6. farmer
7. electrician

B. MATCHING: *WHAT'S THE WORD?*

1. fisherman
2. hairdresser
3. housekeeper
4. foreman

C. OUT OF PLACE!

1. electrician
2. hairdresser
3. construction worker
4. delivery person

WORKBOOK PAGE 83

A. CROSSWORD (see p. 123)

B. LISTENING: *WHO'S TALKING?*

Listen and circle the correct job.

1. I can fix your car this afternoon.
2. Take this medicine every day.
3. May I help you?
4. No problem! I can definitely fix your refrigerator.
5. What color do you want your kitchen?
6. I'm sorry. I can't fix your sink. You need a new one.

Answers

1. mechanic
2. pharmacist
3. salesperson
4. repairperson
5. painter
6. plumber

WORKBOOK PAGE 84

A. WHAT'S THE WORD?

1. welder
2. truck driver
3. taxi driver
4. reporter
5. painter
6. assembler
7. waiter

B. WHICH WORD?

1. secretary
2. taxi driver
3. seamstress
4. stock clerk
5. welder
6. scientist
7. security guard
8. waiter
9. waitress
10. veterinarian

C. LISTENING: *WHO'S TALKING?*

Listen and circle the correct job.

1. I have a very interesting job in a laboratory.
2. For dessert, we have chocolate cake and ice cream. What would you like to order?
3. Here's some medicine for your dog.
4. Hello, Mrs. Benson's office. May I help you?
5. I sit at my sewing machine all day.
6. I meet a lot of people every day. I know the streets of the city very well.

Answers

1. scientist
2. waitress
3. veterinarian
4. secretary
5. seamstress
6. taxi driver

WORKBOOK PAGE 85

A. WHICH WORD?

1. truck
2. assemble
3. grow
4. delivers
5. file
6. build
7. guard
8. mow
9. cook

B. MATCHING: *WHAT DO THEY DO?*

1. c
2. e
3. b
4. f
5. d
6. a
7. k
8. i
9. j
10. h
11. g

WORKBOOK PAGE 86

A. MATCHING: *WHAT DO THEY DO?*

1. d
2. a
3. e
4. c
5. b
6. g
7. j
8. i
9. h
10. f

B. CROSSWORD (see p. 123)

WORKBOOK PAGE 87

A. MATCHING

1. c
2. b
3. e
4. f
5. a
6. d
7. k
8. i
9. g
10. l
11. h
12. j

B. WHICH WORD?

1. mask
2. forklift
3. payroll office
4. freight elevator
5. first-aid kit
6. lever
7. warehouse

C. AT THE FACTORY

1. card
2. clock
3. glasses
4. mask
5. room
6. station
7. line
8. foreman
9. cafeteria
10. machine
11. box

WORKBOOK PAGE 88

A. WHICH GROUP?

Building Materials:	Vehicles:
brick	backhoe
cement	bulldozer
lumber	cement mixer
plywood	dump truck
	front-end loader

B. YES OR NO?

1. Yes
2. No
3. Yes
4. No
5. Yes
6. Yes
7. No
8. No
9. No
10. Yes
11. Yes
12. Yes

C. WHICH WORD?

1. helmet
2. bulldozer
3. pipes
4. wood
5. insulation
6. scaffolding

WORKBOOK PAGE 89

A. WHERE DO THEY GO?

Under the hood:	In the trunk:
battery	flare
carburetor	jack
engine	jumper cables
fan belt	spare tire
radiator	
spark plugs	

B. MATCHING: *WHAT'S THE WORD?*

1. b
2. c
3. a
4. f
5. d
6. e

C. MATCHING: *WHAT CAN THEY USE?*

1.	c	5.	d
2.	g	6.	b
3.	a	7.	f
4.	e		

D. LISTENING: *REPAIR CHECKLIST*

Listen to the repairperson. Check the items that were replaced or fixed.

Mr. Kramer, your car is ready. We checked the spark plugs, and they're fine. We replaced the fan belt, and we also gave you a new carburetor. Your old carburetor had some problems. The battery is in good condition, so we didn't have to replace it. We checked the tires, and they're okay. The rear defroster wasn't working, so we repaired it. Next, we replaced the taillights. They were broken. We checked the windshield wipers. They're working very well, but your headlights weren't working. We replaced both of them. Finally, we checked the radiator, and it had some problems. We tried to fix it, but we couldn't. So we decided to replace it. Do you want to know how much this is going to cost?

Answers

___	spark plugs	✓	rear defroster
✓	fan belt	✓	taillights
✓	carburetor	___	windshield wipers
___	battery	✓	headlights
___	tires	✓	radiator

WORKBOOK PAGE 90

A. MATCHING: *WHAT'S THE WORD?*

1.	c	6.	j
2.	a	7.	f
3.	e	8.	i
4.	d	9.	g
5.	b	10.	h

B. WHAT'S BROKEN?

1.	radio	5.	steering column
2.	speedometer	6.	brakes
3.	rearview mirror	7.	glove compartment
4.	turn signal	8.	visor

WORKBOOK PAGE 91

A. WHICH WORD?

1.	meter	5.	train
2.	subway	6.	conductor
3.	passenger	7.	luggage
4.	turnstile		

B. WHICH WORD DOESN'T BELONG?

1. porter (The others are cars on a train.)
2. timetable (The others are places.)
3. ticket counter (The others are people.)
4. meter (The others are people.)
5. ticket window (The others are related to a taxi.)

C. WHICH WORDS ARE CORRECT?

1.	counter	4.	stand
	window		driver
2.	passenger	5.	schedule
	dining		timetable
3.	station	6.	conductor
	stop		porter

D. LISTENING: *WHERE ARE THEY?*

Listen and circle the correct place.

1. The Los Angeles train is leaving from Track 10. All aboard!
2. A. Excuse me. Where can I get a ticket for the bus to New York?
   B. The ticket counter is over there.
3. A. Can you please take me to 20 Center Street?
   B. 20 Center Street? Sure. No problem.
4. A. Six tokens, please.
   B. Here you are.
5. A. The dining car will open in a few minutes.
   B. Thank you.
6. A. We really need some help with our bags.
   B. There's a porter over there.

Answers

1.	train station	4.	subway
2.	bus station	5.	train
3.	taxi	6.	train station

WORKBOOK PAGES 92–93

A. AT THE AIRPORT

1.	suitcases	11.	detector
2.	ticket	12.	boarding
3.	monitor	13.	check-in
4.	agent	14.	waiting
5.	counter	15.	baggage claim
6.	pass	16.	suitcase
7.	check	17.	garment
8.	checkpoint	18.	customs officer
9.	guard	19.	customs
10.	X-ray		declaration

B. WHICH WORDS ARE CORRECT?

1.	counter	4.	check-in
	agent		ticket
2.	waiting	5.	guard
	baggage claim		checkpoint
3.	customs	6.	area
	immigration		check

C. OUT OF ORDER!

2	2
4	4
6	1
1	6
3	5
5	3
1.	2.

D. WHICH WORD?

1. check-in counter
2. gate
3. customs declaration form
4. passport
5. garment bag

E. LISTENING: *WHERE ARE THEY?*

Listen and choose the correct place.

1. Here's your boarding pass. Your plane leaves from Gate 20 at 3:00.
2. Welcome to the United States. May I see your passport?
3. Please put your bag down on the counter and walk through the metal detector.
4. Here's my suitcase. And here's my garment bag. We can leave the airport now.
5. Your ticket and your boarding pass are fine. You can sit down in the waiting area. We'll be boarding soon.
6. A. Do you have any fruit or vegetables with you?
   B. No, I don't.
   A. Okay. Please open your suitcase.

Answers

1. ticket counter
2. immigration
3. security checkpoint
4. baggage claim area
5. check-in counter
6. customs

WORKBOOK PAGE 94

A. WHICH WORD?

1. cold
2. cloudy
3. foggy
4. windy
5. Winter
6. thunderstorm
7. sleeting
8. cold
9. muggy
10. Fahrenheit, freezing

B. WHICH WORD DOESN'T BELONG?

1. windy (The others refer to temperatures.)
2. thermometer (The others are types of storms.)
3. lightning (The others are types of precipitation.)
4. clear (The others are types of unclear weather.)
5. Fahrenheit (The others are seasons.)

C. LISTENING: *THE WORLD-WIDE WEATHER FORECAST*

Listen to the World-Wide Weather forecast and check *Yes* or *No*.

Hello. This is Gina Jackson with today's World-Wide Weather forecast. It's going to be sunny and warm in France tomorrow. In Spain it's going to be hot and muggy. In Russia you're going to have winter weather. It's going to be cold and windy with temperatures around 20 degrees Fahrenheit. In Sweden there are going to be snowstorms. It's drizzling in Japan right now. That's just the beginning. Tomorrow there are going to be heavy thunderstorms. In Korea it's going to be clear and cool. In the United States we're waiting for a hurricane. Hurricane Charlie is in the Atlantic Ocean today. Tomorrow the hurricane is going to be here in the United States.

Answers

	Yes	No
1.		✓
2.		✓
3.	✓	
4.		✓
5.	✓	
6.		✓
7.	✓	

WORKBOOK PAGE 95

A. WHICH WORD?

1. skiing
2. football
3. fishing
4. bicycling
5. walking
6. swimming sailing

B. CROSSWORD (see p. 124)

C. CROSSWORD

C. CROSSWORD

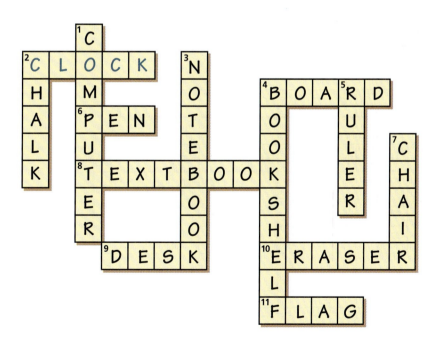

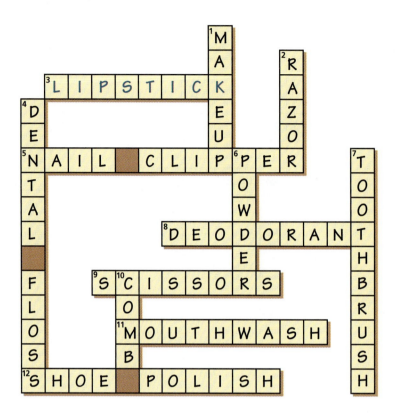

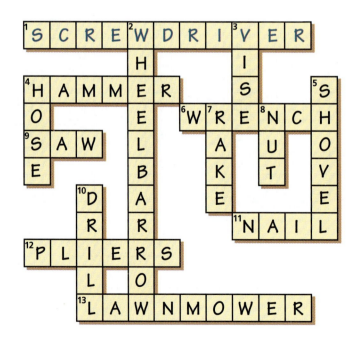

WORKBOOK PAGE 38
B. CROSSWORD

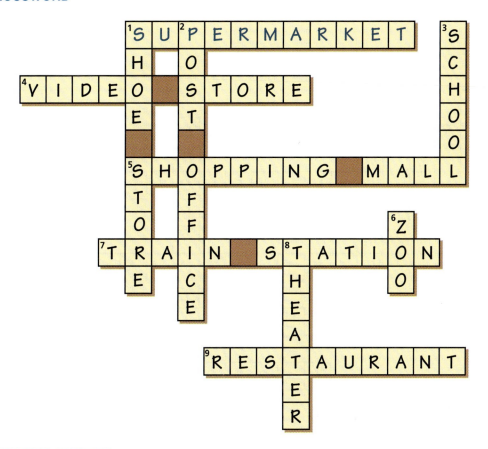

WORKBOOK PAGE 44
A. CROSSWORD

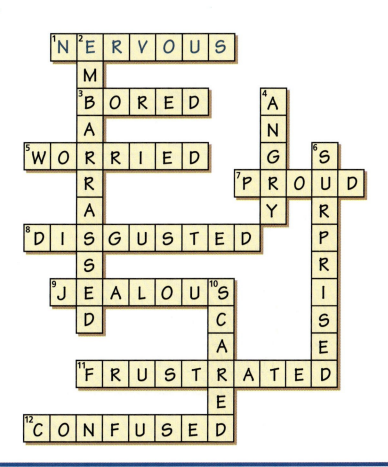

A. CROSSWORD

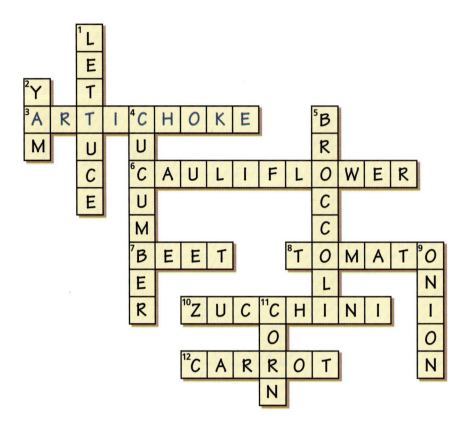

WORKBOOK PAGE 51

B. CROSSWORD

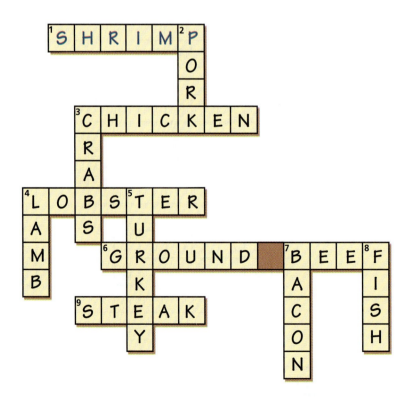

B. CROSSWORD

WORKBOOK PAGE 54

A. CROSSWORD

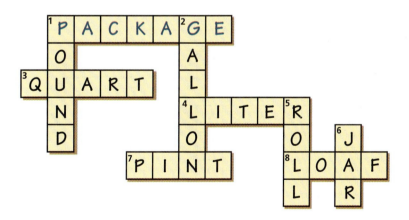

WORKBOOK PAGE 70

D. CROSSWORD

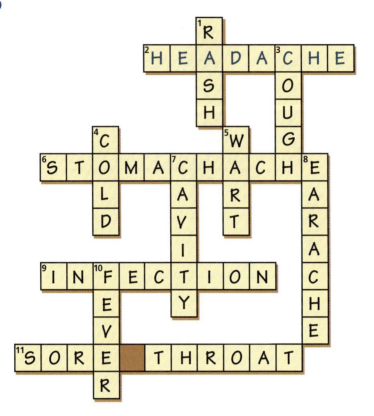

WORKBOOK PAGE 80

A. CROSSWORD

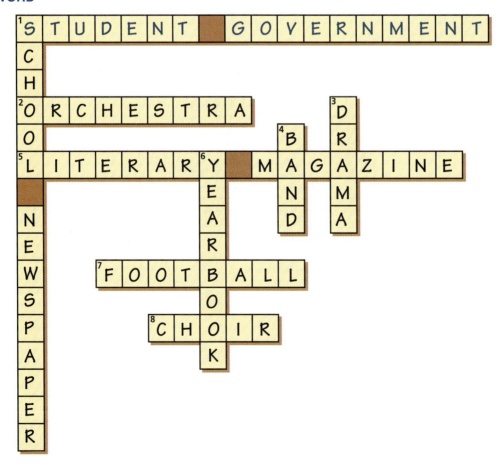

WORKBOOK PAGE 83

A. CROSSWORD

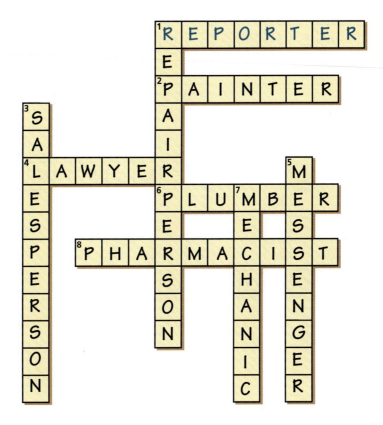

WORKBOOK PAGE 86

B. CROSSWORD

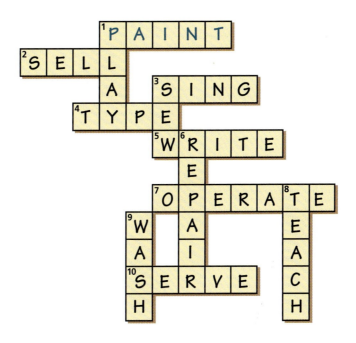

B. CROSSWORD

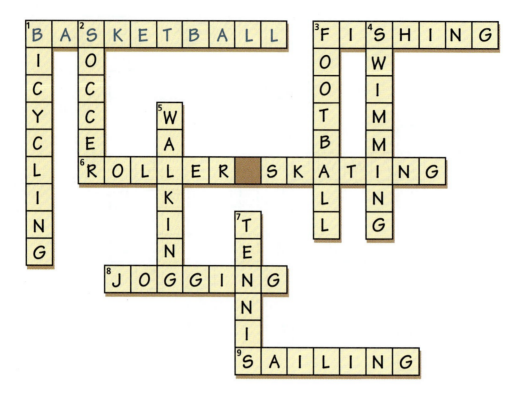